Passing
IPM Ex......

About the author

Elaine Crosthwaite has wide experience in personnel management, education and training, and examining. She is currently the IPM's Manager, Educational Quality, and is responsible for monitoring and approving courses leading to membership of the Institute, at centres throughout the UK.

Prior to joining the IPM, Elaine was Principal Lecturer in Human Resource Management at Nottingham Trent University, and at Coventry University she was the IPM Course Tutor and Associate Head of Department in the Business School. Before coming into higher education, she worked in industry for seven years and was a Personnel Manager for BOC.

Elaine has a Masters degree in Management Studies from Bradford University and is a Fellow of the IPM as well as a member of the ITD. Her previous publications include papers on training, equal opportunities, and personnel management in higher education, and an exam guide for the Open University. She is also the Chief Examiner for the IPM programme at the University of Central England in Birmingham.

Management Studies Series

Series Editors: Michael Armstrong and David Farnham

The IPM examination system through the Professional Management Foundation Programme and the IPM Stage II syllabus provides a unique route into professional personnel practice. The Management Studies Series provides the essential core texts at both levels.

MANAGEMENT STUDIES

Passing Your IPM Exams

Elaine Crosthwaite

Institute of Personnel Management

First published in 1993

© Institute of Personnel Management 1993

Phototypeset by Photoprint, Torquay, Devon
and printed in Great Britain
by Short Run Press, Exeter.

British Library Cataloguing in Publication Data

Crosthwaite, Elaine
 Passing Your IPM Exams. – (Management
 Studies Series)
 I. Title II. Series
 658.3076

ISBN 0–85292–515–8

Contents

v

In memory of my father

Acknowledgements

I want to thank those colleagues who encouraged and assisted me with this book, in particular Derek Torrington and Shelagh Murdoch, and also Andrea Osborne for the typing of the manuscript. Special thanks go to Dave Hall for providing real-life examples and constructive comments on the written draft.

Chapter 1
Introduction

Passing Your IPM Exams is essential reading if:

- you are just embarking on your IPM course of study
- you are looking for some last-minute tips on revision and examination techniques
- you have failed one or more exams and want to know what to do next.

Taking exams is the final step in a learning process that starts on Day 1 of your course. So, this book covers not only revision and exam techniques, but many other topics essential to your success in your IPM course.

First, you should be aware that it is now required that you complete and pass your course work as well as the exams. Therefore several chapters of this book are given over to providing guidance on assessment and on doing course work in the form of assignments and the management report.

Secondly, knowledge of your subject is not a guarantee of success. The other things you need are interest, motivation, study skills, and an ability to apply your knowledge. Therefore this book will give advice on how to analyse case studies, write essays and reports, and gradually practise and develop your skills. It will help you to maximise your returns from the time and effort you put into studying.

Thirdly, you need to be able to apply your knowledge and skills to answering exam questions. This study guide tells you what to expect in each exam and what the examiners are looking for in the answers to questions, so that you can take the approach most likely to lead to success.

Finally, your success will depend on managing your time in the exam so that you complete the right number of questions in the

1

time available. This guide shows you how to plan your answers and get your thoughts down on paper.

Of course, a study guide can't take the place of the face-to-face support and guidance you will get from your tutors, but you should regard it as a supplement to the help and advice available as part of the course of study you have embarked upon. Throughout the study guide, examples are provided to illustrate the approach which it is recommended you take. All the examples are taken from the IPM Education Scheme. So, whether you are on a course leading to IPM national exams, or on a course which has gained approval as meeting the IPM's requirements, you will find the guidance and examples are relevant.

To use your time efficiently, you should choose which chapters to read for your needs as they exist today. At a later stage in your study programme, you may have different needs, and other chapters will be more relevant. If you refer to the list of chapter headings, you will see that the study guide falls roughly into three main parts. Chapters 2, 3, 4 deal with the study and learning skills you will need throughout your programme and should be read at the start of your studies. Chapters 5, 6, 7 deal with specific aspects of the course like the management report and assignments which can be looked up at the relevant time. Chapters 8 and 9 cover the specific skills you will need for taking and passing exams and Chapters 11 to 14 give guidance on the actual content of each of the exams you will be taking.

Chapter 10 will be your starting point if you have completed your course but failed in one or more exams and want to know what help is available and what more you can do to get it right next time. Since failure is often caused not by lack of knowledge or ability, but because inappropriate exam techniques were used, this study guide will provide you with helpful advice on what to do now.

Use the checklist on the next page to work out which chapters you should read at this point in your study programme.

Of course, success in passing your IPM exams also depends on the teaching you receive, the questions which come up on the day, and even your state of health at the time. But, if you follow the guidance given in this book, you should be able to leave less to chance, and be more certain of a happy outcome.

CHAPTERS

I am at:	2	3	4	5	6	7	8	9	10	11	12	13	14
Start of course	√	√	√				√						
First assignment					√	√							
Start of PMFP										√			
Start of Stage 2				√							√	√	√
Exams approaching							√	√					
Something has gone wrong	√								√				

Chapter 2

Surviving the IPM assessment process

The objective of the IPM assessment process is to ensure that everyone who gains Graduate Membership of the IPM has developed the knowledge, skills and professional competence relevant and appropriate to the practice of personnel management in both the immediate and longer-term future. The approved courses of study therefore aim to give you both an understanding of the necessary theories and concepts and a range of practical skills that will help you generally as a manager as well as specifically in operating as a personnel practitioner.

To assess your competences, the courses involve assignments and an organisation-based management report. There are also examinations in order to ensure that students achieve a general standard of work comparable to that of other major qualifications in business and management.

Many students take the IPM's national examinations at Stage 2, and some take these exams at the first stage, too, although at this level the majority of students follow locally assessed programmes. Whatever college or institution you are studying at, you can be sure that your programme has been subject to an approvals process that involves personnel practitioners and tutors from other institutions checking the standards of teaching and learning. Most of the comments in this book will assume that you are taking the IPM's examinations at Stage 2, although we will indicate if there are any major differences you should be aware of on internally assessed programmes.

How the Examination System Works

Chief Examiners and the national examinations

The Chief Examiner for each subject area is responsible for devising the examination paper. The drafted examination papers are considered at an Educational Assessment Committee composed of Chief Examiners, IPM officers and the IPM Vice-President for Membership and Education, to ensure that they are representative of the syllabus and reflect the standards required. The questions are also checked to make sure that students will understand what the examiner wants from them.

After the exam papers have been marked by the team of markers, the Chief Examiner conducts random checks to ensure that scripts have been marked in accordance with the marking scheme, and that the examination system is working correctly. The Educational Assessment Committee then meets to review the examination results and make final decisions on the performance of individual students. At this stage, both assignment and examination results are taken into account in determining whether a student has passed overall. Names of students remain confidential to IPM officers: the examiners do not receive students names with the examination papers, so there is no possibility of bias.

Internally assessed examinations

With these, the examining authority is generally your own course tutors and the exam questions are set under the guidance of the Course Director and Head of Department. External examiners, or moderators, approved by the IPM are appointed to undertake a similar role to the Chief Examiners' in checking exam papers before they are put before students and then checking marked scripts. Each institution has a formally constituted Examination Board at which results are reviewed by tutors and examiners before a decision is made as to whether a student has passed overall.

How exam papers are marked

Students often think that there is an air of mystery surrounding the setting and marking of exam papers. But those responsible for setting exam papers have, like examinees, to justify their proposals! A marking scheme must be prepared by the examiners responsible for setting a question paper. This ensures that:

- The person marking the paper and the Chief or external examiner understands what answer(s) the person who set the paper was seeking.
- The external examiner/moderator of internally assessed courses is able to make an assessment of the standard of the paper in relation to the IPM's requirements.
- The Chief Examiners of nationally assessed courses and external examiners of internally assessed courses are able to check for consistency of marking across a group of examination papers.

We will cover tips on how to approach examinations in Chapter 9 and assignments in Chapter 6, but firstly, we will look in more detail at the education scheme you have embarked upon, the choices you have, and how to get organised as you embark on your course.

The Professional Education Scheme

The structure of the education scheme has been reproduced from the syllabuses and is shown in Appendix A (page 19). As you can see, there are four subject areas in Stage 1, and at Stage 2 students have to study six modules: three core modules plus three generalist modules (or two generalist and one specialist).

You have to complete Stage 1, known as the Professional Management Foundation Programme (PMFP) before you can proceed to Stage 2, because the latter builds on many of the subjects previously studied. For example, the PMFP gives an understanding of the management functions in organisations, how groups work, the importance of costing proposals, interviewing skills, problem-solving, writing reports and making presentations, and all of these are essential for successful study at Stage 2.

Do you have to study for all the exams at once?

The IPM believes that there are enormous advantages in studying the subjects in Stage 1 or Stage 2 in parallel, so that you gain an understanding of the relationships between topics and a wider appreciation of the context in which personnel management operates. At the same time, it is recognised that some students will prefer to study topics in a particular order, perhaps to satisfy more immediate as opposed to longer-term training needs, or because their pace of work may mean that it is not appropriate to take all exams at once. As a result, it is possible to take exams at different sittings.

There are advantages in taking exams all at once which have to be weighed against the advantages of different sittings.

The advantages of taking more than one exam:

- *At PMFP.* The course has been designed as a broad foundation and many of the subjects complement study in another area. For example, there is quite a bit of overlap between Management Processes and Functions and Managing Human Resources in terms of the underlying knowledge about people and organisations.
- *At Stage 2.* There is a compulsory question on each of the three papers which requires the student to draw on and integrate their learning across the three subjects. There is also some overlap between the three subjects, with topics like appraisal systems, disciplinary issues and employee communication and involvement falling into two if not all three subjects.
- Taking exams is stressful whether you are attempting one, two, three or four, but the majority of students pass. Provided you have worked satisfactorily during your course, there is no reason why you should not pass!
- The IPM assessment system gives a 40 per cent weighting to course work and a 60 per cent weighting to exams. Therefore you know how well you are doing as you follow the course, and good course work marks will be taken into account if you have not done very well in the examinations.
- The majority of students take all of their exams at one sitting. Consequently, you will have the benefit of the support which the group can give and be able to maintain the same networks throughout the course.

The advantages of taking exams at different sittings:

- If you have a demanding job, or unforeseen circumstances arise which prevent you studying all subjects concurrently, you can choose which modules to concentrate on in the time you have available.

- If you have not taken exams for many years and are nervous about your ability to learn all there is to know and do your best in the exams, you may choose to take a stepped approach, making use of the May and November sittings.

- You may be taking a related business and management qualification which gives you some accreditation against parts of the IPM programme and you want to obtain the IPM qualification at the same time.

- You are unsure about your commitment and motivation or ability to study to the level required in the IPM course. You may therefore decide to study for those modules which seem more interesting or relevant to your work. In this way, if you do not proceed to gain the full qualification, you will at least have achieved some qualification, rather than none at all.

Generalist versus specialist modules

At Stage 2, specialist modules have been introduced to enable students to study a topic of particular interest to themselves or their organisation. So, for example, a person working in compensation and benefits might prefer to take the Reward Management module, or a training specialist might choose to take the Management Development module. Only one specialist module may be taken in place of one of the three generalist modules in order to ensure that you have a sufficiently broad grounding in the main elements of personnel management.

The IPM has decided that in order to benefit fully from studying a specialist module, students need to have covered the preliminary ground contained in certain core and generalist modules. If you want to take one of the specialist modules therefore, you should ensure that you take the right combination of modules by checking with either your tutor or the IPM Education Department.

Not all centres are approved to offer specialist modules. If your centre does not offer any specialist modules, you may have to follow the standard programme. However, if you are keen, you could explore with your tutor whether arrangements can be made for you to take a specialist module through the IPM's Flexible Learning programme. Alternatively, you could always take an additional module as a continuing professional development activity after you have completed your generalist programme.

Getting Organised

This section will look at the resources available to you as you embark on your course and how to get yourself organised to take advantage of them.

The syllabus

As soon as you enrol as a student member, your Student Information Pack is sent to you, containing the syllabuses and booklists recommended by the Chief Examiners. The vast majority of IPM approved courses will be following the framework provided by the syllabuses, but there are some internally assessed courses which may divide up the topics in a different way. Most institutions provide a student handbook giving the teaching time-table and syllabuses which will be followed, but check with your tutor if you are unsure.

The IPM syllabuses are written in terms of learning objectives and the subject content related to these objectives. From looking at the syllabuses you should be able to identify the essential elements of the course. For example, in Employee Development you will be able to see that there are four principal areas of study, which will be discussed in more detail in Chapter 13. Management Information Systems has three components: finance, statistics and information systems for management decision-making.

The syllabus is a useful guide for a student. At a glance you can see how much of the subject has been covered at any one time, and it also shows the full range of possible areas of assessment, including those elements which might prove to be complex or unattractive to you. At the same time, the syllabus should not be considered as a definitive statement of course content. Individual tutors will want to add up-to-date topics and recent issues which have arisen since the syllabuses were written. Both national examiners and external examiners will provide advice to tutors on current and relevant topics which should be given attention in class. However, the syllabus can be used to check your lecture notes to see if any major parts of the syllabus have not been covered, and if you have any doubts you can check these with your tutors.

Reading and booklists

As mentioned above, your Student Information Pack contains booklists of those texts which the Chief Examiners have recommended for reading. All IPM-approved centres are required to stock these books as a minimum library holding, so you should have no difficulty in obtaining them.

At the start of your course, the amount of reading required can seem daunting, but your tutor can give advice on the most important books to obtain. There will be some which should be purchased as you will need to refer to them frequently, and others which your tutors consider to be background reading and can be obtained from the library.

All the modules in the IPM Professional Education Scheme have a comprehensive textbook dealing with the topics in that subject. Your tutors will be likely to recommend these for purchase but may vary their advice depending on the type of course you are doing. So do ask for advice before you buy any books. Also, student members of the IPM can obtain IPM books at a special discount, and you can save yourself some money if you wait until you have joined the Institute. If you have joined the IPM Flexible Learning programme, you will automatically receive the essential textbooks with your learning materials. Some universities/colleges include the price of essential texts in the course fee so that there is no delay in getting you started on your reading.

Some colleges have a second-hand book shop so you can purchase books used by students in the previous year of the course. These will be for sale at prices substantially lower than normal and should be reasonably up-to-date. If buying second-hand books elsewhere, watch out for old editions as changes in the personnel and employment field can mean books get out of date quickly.

Guided reading is an essential part of your learning. You cannot expect to complete an IPM approved programme by only attending the taught sessions. However, you will rarely have to read a book from cover to cover. Rather, you will use books for a particular purpose, like adding to your lecture notes or background reading for an assignment. Use the library at your university/college as much as possible, and as early as possible, as the most popular texts can be snapped up quickly.

The IPM library

One of the benefits of student membership of the IPM is being able to use the Library and Information Service based at IPM House. It holds the largest collection of personnel management texts and articles in the country and operates a loan or journal photocopy service by telephone and post for a modest fee. You could use the IPM library if a search of your college and local public libraries have not produced the specialist material you require.

When you contact the library do make sure that you have thought through your needs. For example, it is no good asking 'Have you got something on equal opportunities?' You will need to be much more specific to enable the librarian to assist you. There is a standard bibliography already prepared on equal opportunities and many other current topics, which you can obtain if you are at the beginning of your literature search. If your query is more focused, like 'Have you got any notes for guidance on dealing with sexual harassment at work?' you will be in luck as the Library and Information Service has produced a series of codes of conduct. If you are seeking current statistics such as the number of women in top personnel positions, you will find that there is a daily cuttings service, which provides up-to-date information, as well as a wide range of commercially produced surveys by consultants and research institutes.

Personnel management publications

Once you are a registered student, each month you will receive your copy of *Personnel Management* and *PM Plus*. These are a valuable resource, as they contain up-to-the-minute articles summarising research in specialist fields and giving examples of good practice in personnel management. Particularly in the areas of employment legislation, national training arrangements, and international personnel management, you will find you need to support your reading of textbooks by reading current articles and news items. The personnel management publications will be one of your principal sources of information.

Past examination papers and examiners' reports

Whether you are taking IPM national or internally assessed exams, you can obtain copies of past exam papers. For the national exams you can get copies of the 'specimen exam paper', recent exam papers and the examiners' reports for any subject from the IPM Education Department. In many cases tutors will give out this information to students as part of their introduction to the topic.

If you are at an internally assessed centre, the past exam papers should be available either from the Examinations Office, or perhaps from the Students' Union office. There may be a small charge but if you can, get together with a small group of students to share the papers.

It is essential that you familiarise yourself with the format of the exam and the type of questions set. Check the questions against the topics listed in the syllabus and see which tend to appear more frequently.

You can analyse IPM examiners' reports to find out the approach the examiner is looking for. The reports indicate the major errors made in examinees' answers with regard to every question that appeared on the previous exam paper. They do not actually give you the answer that the examiner was expecting, but they do provide a great deal of detailed guidance about what is required when you answer exam questions.

Included in the examiner's report are the pass and failure rates for the examination. Typically, about two-thirds of candidates pass. This should give you an incentive to concentrate on your studies and revision. The reports also give an indication of what to look out for to avoid adding to the fail statistics! Many of the comments on examination preparation in this book have been drawn from past examiners' reports, and you will find that the same errors and omissions catch students out year after year.

The 'specimen examination paper' indicates the likely coverage of the examination for each subject and gives tutors and students an idea of the way questions are likely to be phrased. Occasionally specimen answers for an examination question are provided. They are useful as an indication of the standard of work required, although they should not be regarded as ideal or model answers. We have reproduced specimen questions and answers in later sections.

Tutors

Your tutors are, of course, a resource, but the exact nature of the support you can expect will depend upon the type of programme you are following. On IPM Flexible Learning programmes, the tutors will have agreed a learning contract with each student and have undertaken to provide telephone and face-to-face tuition and guidance at certain times. On taught courses, you may or may not have entered into a learning contract, but you should be given a class timetable and a student handbook which outlines the people and facilities provided to help you on the course. If you are not clear about the course requirements, an item in your study packs or something the tutor says, do not hesitate to ask for an explanation.

Tutors are just as keen that you get through the exams as you are. High pass rates reflect well on individual tutors and courses in general. Low or mediocre pass rates are likely to attract the critical attention of external examiners and, in the case of the IPM national examinations, repeatedly poor results will result in a review by the Institute's Education Quality Assurance Panel.

Tutors will provide you with handouts, although this is one area where there is no satisfying everybody! Some students complain that there are too many handouts to read, while others will say they do not get enough. What you can expect is that a tutor will give you a handout when it is an effective use of your time to read rather than take down notes in a lecture. This may be because the ideas and concepts are complex and more easily conveyed by the written word, or because the handout contains a detailed case study or example of practice which is not central but a useful addition to your knowledge. Sometimes tutors will give you a handout of key points as a conceptual scaffold for the topic they are about to cover. Whichever, you should not just grunt and stuff the handout into a pile of papers as many students have been observed to do, but clarify the purpose of the handout and make use of it in the manner intended.

Some students expect their tutor to be the fount of all knowledge and are disappointed if they leave a session with few notes. Hopefully, after reading the chapter on learning they will realise that learning comes from a variety of stimuli, only one of which is the tutor. Tutors are only human and will have a range of knowledge and experience which qualifies them to teach on the course, but they cannot hope to know the answer to every question you may put. They also feel just as nervous when standing in front of a class for the first time as you do when you start on a new course. Therefore striking up a good relationship with your tutors will be mutually beneficial, and will contribute to a more valuable learning experience. Talk to your tutors informally before or after a session, and invite them for a coffee or a drink after class.

On your course you can expect a mix of teaching and learning methods, particularly role playing, case studies and discussion, as well as lectures and demonstrations, and the use of computers, video and CCTV as teaching tools. We will cover more on learning from case studies in a later chapter, but we will now go on to consider the ways in which you can get the most out of group working with fellow students.

Fellow students

As well as getting to know your tutor, getting to know other students on the course will help your learning experience. Not only will you look forward to attending all the lessons, but you will get more out of them if you feel at ease.

Most students who come together on the first day of a course are strangers, and tutors will usually organise an 'ice-breaking' activity in order to begin the process of getting to know each other. One common method is to get each student to interview the person sitting alongside and then to introduce them to the rest of the group. Thus, each individual talks to at least one other person and the group gets to know about each of its members.

The introductions normally cover details such as work experience, educational background, leisure interests and why the course has been chosen. You will probably find that somebody else in the group has a number of things in common with you. It is well worth listening carefully to the introductions and making a few notes so that when you are asked to get into small groups for later activities, you can choose to work with students with similar needs or interests. Social cohesiveness in a group has benefits. With a relaxed group, classroom discussion is less inhibited, clarification can more readily be sought and information can be analysed and evaluated more effectively.

Working in groups

On your course you will be encouraged to study in groups and some of your assessments may be based on group work. The reason for using group work is that a group can develop a wider and deeper understanding of a topic through the pooling and questioning of ideas. In addition, in organisations we all work in groups, so you can use the group working sessions as a vehicle for developing your own skills and personnel effectiveness.

There are five main situations in which you will encounter group work on your course:

- *Discussion groups*. Your tutor will often present a set of ideas and ask you to consider these for their practical application. The group may be asked to provide a spokesperson to report on the group's findings to the rest of the class. Alternatively, an informal group may get together to hold a constructive and free-ranging discussion on a specific topic or question. The value of this is immense and will be dealt with below in the section headed 'Self-help groups'.
- *Brainstorming*. There may not be time to hold a free-ranging discussion and you may be asked to put forward as many facts or ideas on a topic or question as can be thought of within a given period of time. The major points from the pool of ideas will then be extracted and agreed.
- *Case study work*. A group will be formed to examine a case or resolve a problem, for example to consider how the personnel department of a rapidly expanding company should be structured and staffed. Often each group presents its conclusions to the rest of the class, or alternatively the exercise will be written

up as an assignment. Case study work is a valuable experience and preparation for the case study questions in the examinations.

- *Role-playing.* In role-play situations, a group of students work towards the solution of a problem by each playing a role so that the procedure simulates a possible real life situation. This can be a very enjoyable and powerful method of learning both the subject matter and how to handle awkward situations such as interviewing a recalcitrant employee.
- *Seminars and tutorials.* Seminars will normally be organised and conducted by the tutor and are very useful in developing a student's ability to analyse problems. Often a class member will be asked to prepare a paper and the seminar will involve discussion of the ideas presented. So they are basically discussion groups with the purpose and momentum controlled by the tutor. Tutorials are more like small group teaching situations and will tend to be more open and free-ranging.

Depending on the type of course you are on, there will be varying opportunities for group work. If your course is full-time, you will find there is a large amount of group work. If your course is part-time the proportion is likely to be smaller, but there will be possibilities of supplementing formal group work with informal *self-help groups*.

Benefits and difficulties of group work

We indicated above that there are positive benefits from group work. In some groups of students, quite a high level of cooperation is achieved, with 'experts' coaching weaker members, books and articles being shared and revision sub-groups being set up.

However, effective groups do not 'just happen': they have to be worked at. You will learn about group formation and development in Managing Human Resources, but in brief, the needs of the task, team and the individual need to be met. If good progress towards achieving the task is not made, then members will become disenchanted. However, equally importantly, the social needs of group members must be met. Members must have a rapport with each other, feel recognised and valued as members. You may find yourself assigned to a group, in which case you will have to work with the constraints imposed by the group's composition. But, if you have a choice, there are several factors you may wish to consider.

Choosing a group

- *Size of group.* The optimum size of group will depend on the task, but for most IPM projects and activities between four and six members is likely to be most appropriate. Larger groups present logistical problems of finding convenient times to get together. A smaller group may have less resources of knowledge and experience to draw on, and there will be fewer pairs of hands to divide up the work. For example, if you are given the task of designing and delivering an instructional session to the rest of your class, or researching the business environment of a major company, you will probably find that four members will be adequate. If you are setting up an informal self-help group, you will probably find six members bring in a wider range of expertise and more resources.
- *Composition.* There will be a tendency to work with people from a similar background to your own. In order to get a wide perspective on the tasks and problems you work on, it can be more beneficial to join a group from a variety of backgrounds with a range of expertise. For example large and small company, public and private sector, line management and personnel specialist experience can all contribute to a different perspective and understanding of the issues and their implications.

  Tensions can arise if some members of the group are more hardworking and others seem to want to do the minimum to pass. The resolution of such conflicts is a valuable learning experience, but if the group's effectiveness is impaired and assessed course work is involved, you should raise the problem with your tutor.

  An informal or an appointed leader is likely to exist in all groups. There is an advantage in having someone who takes on the responsibility of getting everybody together at the right time, and who can get group members to contribute towards achieving the group's objectives. It is preferable if a group actually chooses a chairperson because they think he or she is capable of fulfilling that role.

Self-help groups

You will be encouraged to form a self-help group to assist you in your studies. If you are on the IPM Flexible Learning programme, your tutors will take steps to help you form networks for mutual support. On most programmes, tutors will advise you of the benefits of sharing information and pooling your resources.

Most students will have two or three classmates whom they can telephone for support and encouragement when they feel the need. Some students, especially on part-time programmes, will meet regularly to discuss their approach to assignments and for revision purposes.

Whatever the basis of your self-help group, you will find the following guidelines useful in establishing and running an effective group:

- Share personal details and telephone numbers so that you can contact each other easily outside of the formal programme.
- Decide on the objectives of your self-help group, for example:
  −discussion of the next assignment
  −mutual support for a subject which you find diffcult, e.g. Management Information Systems
  −revision study group.
- Agree on the topic for discussion at the next meeting and what preparation would be useful beforehand.
- Decide when to meet, and for how long, and organise a suitable venue with appropriate facilities, access to refreshments, etc. The pub might be a good place for an initial meeting, but your meetings will be more productive in an appropriate venue.
- Appoint a coordinator or chairperson who can be the main contact point and will take the initiative in organising the first few meetings.
- At the start of the meeting, check your objectives and decide on the most appropriate way of working in order to achieve these objectives. Review the operation of the group at the end of the meeting and see if there are any implications for future meetings.

Appendix A

Structure of the education scheme

The scheme is divided into two stages. There are four subject areas in Stage 1, the Professional Management Foundation Programme. At Stage 2 students have to study six modules: three core modules and three chosen from the nine remaining modules, of which at least two must be generalist modules. As part of this stage students complete six assignments and one management report, which form a part of the final assessment for the course.

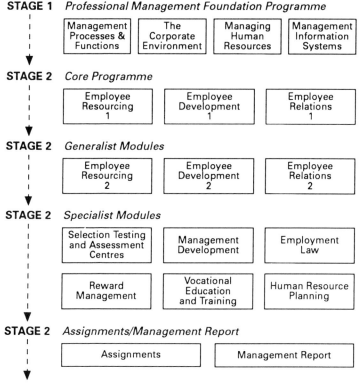

STAGE 1 *Professional Management Foundation Programme*

| Management Processes & Functions | The Corporate Environment | Managing Human Resources | Management Information Systems |

STAGE 2 *Core Programme*

| Employee Resourcing 1 | Employee Development 1 | Employee Relations 1 |

STAGE 2 *Generalist Modules*

| Employee Resourcing 2 | Employee Development 2 | Employee Relations 2 |

STAGE 2 *Specialist Modules*

| Selection Testing and Assessment Centres | Management Development | Employment Law |
| Reward Management | Vocational Education and Training | Human Resource Planning |

STAGE 2 *Assignments/Management Report*

| Assignments | Management Report |

Graduate of the Institute of Personnel Management

Chapter 3

Understanding how you learn

We all have very distinct styles of learning and vary in the learning skills we can bring to bear when faced with a learning opportunity. The term 'learning styles' is used as a description of the attitudes and behaviours which determine an individuals' preferred way of learning. Most people have a vague idea of their learning style preferences because they feel more comfortable in some learning situations than others. In this chapter we shall give a brief introduction to learning styles and ways of improving your learning processes.

Learning Styles

During your study of both the PMFP and Employee Development, you should find that your tutors refer to learning styles. There are a number of different models, but the most well known are those of Kolb, and Honey and Mumford. Kolb's cycle of learning[1] involves four key stages of:

- concrete experience
- reflective observation
- abstract conceptualisation
- active experimentation

. . . and a learning experience is only fully effective when all the main stages have been planned and followed.

Honey and Mumford have suggested that individuals prefer to learn in different ways, broadly related to the four Kolb stages, and have developed a learning styles questionnaire to help people identify their preferred learning style. You may have already completed this questionnaire, but if not, you are recommended to obtain *The Manual of Learning Styles*[2] which contains the questionnaire, score sheets and guidelines on using the approach in learning and training situations. Even if you have previously completed the questionnaire, it is useful to revisit it periodically to check whether you are 'learning to learn' and have developed a wider range of learning styles.

The following statements give a broad indication of the type of response you may make in a learning situation:

1. 'I'll try anything once.'
2. 'I need some time to think about this.'
3. 'How does this fit with that?'
4. 'How can I use this in my job?'

Each of the statements is indicative of a different learning style. You may think that more than one is typical of you, and you may even think that all responses are possible depending on the situation you are in. However, there are usually one or two styles which we tend to use more often than others, and it is helpful to understand how we tend to learn at present so we can see what opportunities for learning we are overlooking or not maximising. On the other hand, knowing which type of learning activities you do not find particularly valuable will help you to understand why some parts of the IPM programme are tedious or frustrating and others are interesting and stimulating.

The following descriptions relate to the four learning styles identified by Honey and Mumford, and examples are given of the types of activities which you can undertake to complement your learning style and make learning seem easier!

Activist

Typical reactions of Activists to learning situations are:

'I'll try anything once.' (*Statement 1*)
'If it goes wrong, we can put it down to experience.'
'I get bored with methodical, detailed work.'

Activists are open-minded people who welcome new experiences. They often tackle problems by brainstorming and will tend to be weaker on implementation or anything requiring sustained effort.

If you are an Activist you will be quite happy to be thrown in at the deep end with a difficult task. You will enjoy activities such as role playing and competitive team-work tasks. If your group is asked to appoint someone to chair a discussion or give a presentation, you will be quite happy to be put in the spotlight.

You are likely to get 'fed up' if your course involves too much time listening to lectures, or a lot of reading, writing and thinking on your own. Too much emphasis on case analysis and discussions will not appeal to you and although project work may be enjoyable, you will be irked by the length of time and need to structure the process.

Reflector

Typical reactions of Reflectors to learning situations are:

> 'I need some time to think about this.' (*Statement 2*)
> 'I like to listen to other people's points of view before putting my own forward.'
> 'It worries me if I have to rush a piece of work to meet a tight deadline.'

Reflectors are thoughtful people who like to consider all possible angles and enjoy observing other people in action.

If you are a Reflector you will be quite happy collecting and analysing data, probing to get to the bottom of things and producing carefully prepared reports. You prefer structured learning experiences and can sometimes find classes are not well organised. You will not relish being forced to role play or act as a leader/chairperson or being rushed from one activity to another. You enjoy analysing case studies, observing others, and can be a good source of feedback, but will prefer it if someone else presents the results of small group work to the rest of the class.

Theorist

Typical reactions of Theorists to learning situations are:

> 'How does this fit with that?' (*Statement 3*)
> 'I like to explore the basic assumptions, principles and theories underpinning things.'
> 'I find it difficult to produce ideas on impulse.'

Theorists are analytical people who prefer to work through problems in a logical way rather than rely on subjective judgements.

If you are a Theorist you will want to know the justification for a particular line of thought or argument, who did the research, and whether their methodology was sound. Equally, you will be happy to listen to or read about ideas and concepts which are logical and well argued, even if they have no immediate use to you. You will thrive on the more academic aspects of the course.

You will not like participating in activities which emphasise emotions and feelings or being 'thrown in' to situations without a clear purpose. For example, you will not relish practising different stances in interpersonal skills exercises, but you will like the opportunity to be stretched by a complex problem in your Management Report.

Pragmatist

Typical reactions of Pragmatists to learning situations are:

'How can I use this in my job?' (*Statement 4*)
'I like to learn about new techniques like neuro-linguistic programming.'
'In discussions I get impatient with irrelevances and digressions.'

Pragmatists are practical types who are keen to try out new ideas and techniques to see if they work in practice.

If you are a Pragmatist you will look for the link between the subject you are studying and a problem or opportunity at work. You enjoy learning in situations where there is a credible expert or coach who can demonstrate how things should be done.

You will be impatient with open-ended discussions which seem to be 'waffling' around subjects and not reaching practical solutions and plans. You will also find it difficult to listen and learn if you cannot see the immediate benefit or relevance of the topic being studied. Case studies showing how other organisations have solved problems, and skills development activities provided you get helpful feedback, will appeal to you. You will respond to mentoring provided your mentor is a respected, authoritative figure.

The diagram below shows how each learning style connects with the stages of the learning cycle.

People with Activist preferences are well prepared for experiencing, while Reflectors are more inclined to reflect on their observations or experiences. People with Theorist preferences like to form concepts and are well equipped for concluding, while Pragmatists are more disposed to planning and experimenting.

You will be more effective as a learner if you are aware of your learning style preferences and the activities which are related to your style. You may find that you are missing out on some activities which ought to be attractive to you. However, you should not avoid those activities which do not accord with your preferred style(s). Since a learning experience is only fully effective when *all* the main stages have been completed, you must not only make the best use of your strengths, but must try to develop those styles you do not currently use, in order to become an all-round learner.

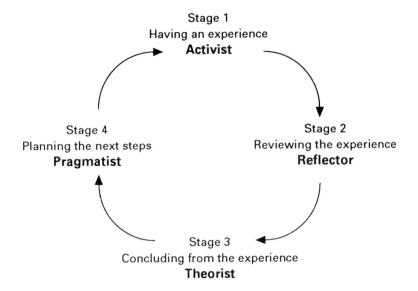

Stage 1
Having an experience
Activist

Stage 4
Planning the next steps
Pragmatist

Stage 2
Reviewing the experience
Reflector

Stage 3
Concluding from the experience
Theorist

Improving Your Learning Processes

An understanding of learning styles can help in improving your learning processes, but there are other aspects of learning which can cause problems. These generally stem from two sources: learning blockages and learning methods.

Learning blockages

We all have 'blockages' – mental, emotional or intellectual – which can hamper our learning. Fear of making a fool of yourself can prevent you from volunteering to give a presentation on behalf of your group or taking part in a role play. As a consequence, you miss out on a valuable opportunity for learning. Many students on IPM courses are convinced that they are no good at statistics. Often they have come from an educational background where they avoided numerical subjects and when faced with Management Information Systems they doubt their ability to learn the subject. It is interesting to note that the pass rate in this module is not too different from that of other modules. Learning blockages can be overcome.

Mental blockages can often affect thought processes and the ability to solve problems. Try the following exercise, which is based on the game BOGGLE (Registered tradename of Parker Brothers). The objective is to list within three minutes as many words of four letters or more as you can find in the grid. Words are formed from adjoining letters in the proper sequence. They may

U	A	N	O	H
E	R	E	S	R
R	K	T	A	P
S	D	T	I	N
D	S	S	L	E

join horizontally, vertically or diagonally; to the left, right or up and down. Ignore plurals and the names of places or persons, e.g. Spain, Rhone. Examples of words in the grid above are pattern, earnest, treason, prose and kettle. You should be able to get up to 15 words in three minutes (or even more). Start now.

You will find a list of about 90 words which can be formed from the letters in Appendix B (page 30). Now review how you tackled the task.

Did you find it easy to make associations? How did you get started – did you jump around the grid or did you try to structure your approach by looking for groups of letters which gave you a nucleus, e.g. SA, PA, STR and then look for adjacent letters? Did you concentrate in one area and build? Or did you keep trying out different ideas? Did you turn the grid around and look at it from a different angle – for example, the word SAIL can be clearly seen from one angle.

Now what do you conclude about your approach to this exercise? What does it tell you about your thought processes? Do you try to look at things from different perspectives? In problem solving do you consider other possibilities to see if they might be appropriate as solutions?

What have you learned about your approach to learning and problem solving which you can apply in other situations?

Incidentally, if you skipped doing the exercise at all, what has that told you about your learning style preferences?

Learning methods

Another problem in learning is that you may be trying to learn by using methods which are not compatible with the way your brain works. Most people have learnt to learn by trial and error – teachers at school did not teach you how to use your brain effectively! So, just as when you teach yourself to work a new video, computer or piece of equipment, you form bad habits and conclude that this is due to the equipment, not the user, so too with the way your brain works in relation to study. You can use your brain more effectively. One way is the method by which you take notes and we shall consider this later. Here we discuss what happens when you learn something new.

The brain assimilates new information by establishing connections between new information and already known information. Fortunately, there are many well-known memory techniques which can help you make these connections and then retain and recall the material that you need to remember. We will look at these shortly, but firstly, concentration is important and there are a number of factors which can assist good concentration and good remembering.

- *Attitude to work.* A positive approach is essential – people who are interested in a topic have little difficulty in remembering quite complicated details. Hopefully, you are doing your IPM course because you are interested in the subject matter, but there may be other factors preventing good remembering.
- *Attitude of mind.* If you are anxious or under stress your concentration will be much reduced, and so too your chance of retaining and recalling what you are trying to learn. Try to resolve the anxiety or stress before you start to study so you have a clear mind.
- *Realistic goals.* Set yourself realistic goals for a study session. A 30-minute period of concentrated and productive work is better than two hours with frequent interruptions for a reluctant student.
- *Structure.* When you are presented with new material try to identify a clear pattern, structure or relationships. The act of classifying and structuring disorganised material assists the memory and learning processes.
- *Key words.* As their name implies, key words help recall.

To illustrate the last two points, try the following exercise:

Read and try to remember the following words:

case study, labour turnover, discipline, role play, lecture, stability index, counselling, selection, discussion, age distribution

As they are, the words are not easy to remember, but if the words are grouped, or classified, it becomes much easier to remember the items in each group and recall them later. For example:

Training techniques: case study, role play, lecture, discussion

Types of interviews: discipline, counselling, selection

Workforce analysis: labour turnover, stability index, age distribution

The association of ideas also enables you to make a reasonable guess at any missing items.

At some point in your studies you will have to learn key points or facts. So, when you are trying to learn, there are three basic ways of remembering facts:

- *Context*. Learning groups of items will be useless if you cannot place them in the correct context. You can probably remember the ten words in the exercise above because they relate to your IPM studies and you can put them into a structure.
- *Repetition*. Either by reading a passage many times or by repeating material to yourself, preferably aloud. You probably learnt your 'tables' in this way at school. If you put the material in your own words, either in writing or by speaking aloud, repetition will be even more effective.
- *Mnemonics*. Mnemonics is a term for a device to help us recall items. During our education we have used mnemonics often to help our memory. These are some examples:

  –Rhymes

  You learnt to spell words like receive by reciting 'I before E, except after C'

  You learnt the number of days in the month from the rhyme 'Thirty days hath September . . .'

  –Visual images

  Visual association is useful for remembering one or two words by linking them with an object. It does not matter how stupid or simple the link but it does help if it is amusing. So, we remember that stalagmites grow up (bishop's mitre) and stalactites come down (as do tights).

  –Making up words/sentences

  One of the easiest ways to remember a list of facts is simply to take the first letter of each of the words you have to remember and make them into another word or a sentence. We remember the colours of the rainbow in the following way:

Richard	Red
Of	Orange
York	Yellow
Gave	Green
Battle	Blue
In	Indigo
Vain	Violet

We can remember the four learning styles identified by Honey and Mumford by arranging the first letter of each word to form the word PART:

Pragmatist
Activist
Reflector
Theorist

As each person's imagination and experience are unique, different methods will work better for different people. You should try out and use those ways of remembering which work best for you.

References

1. KOLB, D.A., RUBIN, I.M. and McINTYRE, J.M. *Organisational Psychology: An experiential approach.* 1974
2. HONEY, P. and MUMFORD, A. *The Manual of Learning Styles.* 1992

Appendix B

Learning Exercise Checklist

ARSON	PARSON	SERE
DREAR	PAST	SETTLE
EARN	PASTE	SHONE
EARNEST	PATE	SITE
EAST	PATER	SITTER
ELITE	PATTER	SLIP
ENLIST	PATTERN	SLIT
HONE	PILE	SNARE
HONEST	PINE	SNEAR
HORSE	PRATE	SONAR
HOSE	PRATTLE	SPAN
HOST	PRONE	SPAR
HOSTILE	PROSE	SPAT
KERN	RAIL	SPATE
KETTLE	RAIN	SPIN
LIAR	RAPINE	SPINE
LIEN	RASH	SPIT
LINE	RATE	SPRAIN
LIST	RATTLE	SPRAT
LITTER	REAP	STAIN
NAIL	REAR	STAR
NEAR	REASON	STASH
NEAT	REST	STATE
NEST	RETAIL	STERN
NETT	RETAIN	STILE
NETTLE	ROSE	TAIL
NORSE	ROSTER	TEAR
NOSE	SAIL	TENOR
PAIL	SANE	TERN
PAIN	SATE	TILE
PANE	SATIN	TREASON
PANEL	SEAR	TREAT
PARSE	SEAT	TREK

Chapter 4

Learning faster with less effort

To learn faster with less effort, you will need to develop skills in time management, reading, listening and note-making. This chapter tackles these crucial elements of successful study.

Time Management

If you want to be successful in your studies, you will need to think through how to use your time efficiently. If you are following a Flexible Learning programme, your tutors will give you a study planner with an indication of the timetable you should follow in order to cover the material. But you will still need to think through how to fit in work, study, leisure and domestic commitments.

If you are on a taught course, you will be given a timetable of tutor-run sessions, but you will need to devote the same amount of time to study outside class as in, and this will require planning and organising. Whichever study method you have chosen you need to plan your workload so that you can cover all your studies, integrate them into your normal lifestyle, both at home and at your place of work, and remain sane.

The skills you need to manage your learning are the same as any manager needs in planning and organising their work: goal-setting and then measuring progress along the path to the goal you have set yourself. In addition, there are a number of aspects of time management which are particular to studying for your IPM qualification, and this chapter will provide some general guidelines on planning and managing your study time.

A study plan

Almost all students describe shortage of time as a problem. For part-time students the problem is particularly acute, as time for study has to be 'found' either by ceasing to do some things you are presently doing, or doing some things more efficiently, or both! Time for study will have to be negotiated with work colleagues and family if your physical and emotional well-being is to be maintained.

You should receive a programme of dates for submission of assignments and your tutors should be able to guide you on the amount of study time needed. On a Flexible Learning course this will be about 15 hours per week, while on a part-time taught course, this is likely to be at least six hours on top of the time attending classes.

One way of determining how you can find the time required is to map out a diary for a typical week on a sheet of A4 paper. The chart shown on the next page can be used to plan out your weekly timetable.

To produce your own chart on a piece of paper, put the days of the week down the side and the hours along the top of the chart. Fill in the spaces with your essential activities like eating, travelling, work and shopping, then enter your other commitments and see how much time you have left for study.

You will need to consider three aspects:

- How much time you expect to need for study based on the guidance given by your tutors.
- How much time you have available. You may be able to identify some activities which could be sacrificed altogether for the period of your studies, some which could be reduced, and some which perhaps could be done more efficiently. Do not, however, stop all of the things you enjoy doing, as relaxation and physical well-being are essential for productive and effective study.
- Freeing the additional time you need. Cutting down on watching TV and leisure activities are obvious ways of freeing time and it is likely to be necessary to cut down on an active social life. You could also experiment with gradually cutting back on sleep and getting up earlier or going to bed later than usual in order to make time available to study.

What is important is to set yourself a timetable that is realistic, not over-demanding, and schedule in some relaxation and time to enjoy yourself.

A weekly planner alone will not be sufficient. You will need a

Day	6	7	8	9	10	11	12	13	14	15	16	17	18	19	20	21	22	23	24
Mon		Brkfst & Travel			At Work				Lunch self help grp	At Work			Travel	Meal	Prepare Notes			Relax	
Tues		Jog	Brkfst & Travel		At Work			Lunch		At Work			Travel	Meal	Leisure				
Wed	Plan project		Brkfst & Travel		At Work			Lunch		At Work			Travel	Meal	Prepare for College				
Thurs		Jog	Brkfst & Travel		At Work			Lunch & Travel		College							Travel	Relax	
Fri			Brkfst & Travel		At Work			Lunch with staff		At Work			Travel	Shopping		Meal	Relax		
Sat		Jog	Brkfst 3 hours work following college					Lunch Family						Theatre					
Sun			Brkfst	Family						Work on assignment					Family and TV				

Adapted from G.E. Sutcliffe[1]

longer-term study planner. For this a wall planner is particularly useful as you will be able to see comparative time factors very clearly. The dates for submission of assignments and projects, as well as workshops, residentials and examinations can be inserted. A personal study plan will enable you to make sure that you have all the books and notes ready for an individual study session, and can maximise your use of the time allocated. The advantage of this approach is that you have set targets to achieve and consequently benefit from the feeling of well-being on achieving your targets and making clear progress in your studies.

When to study

There has been much research on this subject and no time is right for everyone. Some people can study better at night and others prefer early mornings. You will also find that to some extent the available time slots in your study plan dictate when you have to study.

However, there are a range of activities included in studying: planning, information gathering, reading, memorising, note-taking, and writing. You may find that you are better at certain activities at different times of the day and can arrange your studies accordingly.

Having a regular time to study can be advantageous. If you always go to study at set times family and friends know your pattern and what to expect, and it takes away the pain of deciding whether or not to study on a particular occasion.

Where to study

There are obvious practical advantages of having a place devoted to study. You will be accumulating a significant volume of notes and will be working on assignments which take several sessions to complete. You need somewhere where you can leave your materials and notes and easily locate all the things you require without shuffling through heaps of paper. The ideal is a room used exclusively for studying, where you can work without being subjected to too many distractions. Some people prefer to study in their workplace, provided they have access outside normal working hours. If you are unable to find a permanent space of your own to study in, then you should at least invest in some box files to keep your materials together.

On the other hand, the danger of having a really good place to study is that you might ignore other opportunities. There are not many things you can only do when you have all your materials to hand. You need to try to make studying part of your whole life. For example, driving to work can be a good time to listen to a tape on a cassette player in the car. You can read some pages of a textbook and test yourself mentally while travelling on public transport, and a little gentle revision of material you've already covered can be done almost anywhere.

How to study

Irrespective of when you choose to study, your span of attention will dictate how long you can concentrate without a break. In lectures, tutorials and workshops, tutors will make allowances for this, and you must do the same in your self-study periods. Although each individual varies, a good rule of thumb is to take a five-minute break in every hour. During this time it is a good idea to get up, move around a little and perhaps make a cup of coffee, but do not distract your mind to outside matters. While you take this short physical break, your subconscious will still be considering the material being thought about, and often a point will become clearer. After taking a brief break, look over the material you have been working on, and after this short review, you will be ready to start your next period of intensive study.

When you find yourself getting bored with an activity such as reading, try setting yourself a question to answer, or sketch out a plan for your next assignment. If however, you find you are just not taking things in, then stop and return later – a bored brain does not absorb things well.

Maintaining momentum

Even if you have planned your time, where and when to study, and ensured that there will be no interruptions, your motivation will flag as the novelty of studying wears off. A sense of achievement is vital in maintaining your level of interest. One useful way of gaining this is to split your work into 'bite-sized chunks' and reward yourself with a treat at the end of each chunk. This could be a cup of coffee or a snack at the end of each chunk. If you have a wall chart or a timetable on which to tick off the various activities you have completed, this should help your motivation as well as being a good control device. Another tip to use at the end of a study session is always to leave everything ready for the next session, so that you can get going immediately.

If you compare notes with others in your study group you will probably find that they have similar problems in maintaining motivation and interest. As human beings our moods change and we have ups and downs. Many students will go through periods when self-doubt comes to the surface and dominates their thoughts. This can happen when you feel under pressure, or a low assignment grade and a domestic problem come together and generate anxiety.

To deal with such feelings, it is important to remind yourself that before starting this course, you underwent a selection procedure in which you demonstrated that you have the necessary ability. The course is designed as a series of steps towards success! However, if you feel that problems are building up, talk to the Course Director. If you are having workload problems, talk to the subject tutor or Course Director before deadlines are past. Provided you can show that you have taken a conscientious approach to your studies, you will find that your tutors will do all they can to help you.

Reading

Your IPM course will involve extensive reading. If you are on a Flexible Learning course you have chosen to work on your own through a range of written learning materials. On a class-based course you will also have to read background literature and sources in preparation for assignments.

Of all the skills needed for effective learning, reading is the most significant and yet it is often done inefficiently.

How are you using this book?

Hopefully, you are using the Contents List to direct you to the sections you need most.

Many students will be reading this book slowly and carefully, working through from beginning to end, and making notes or underlining the main points as they go. For three reasons, this may not be effective.

- Titles can be deceptive and a relevant-sounding title may precede something which is of little interest or relevance. Therefore you should first quickly scan the item. If it is a book, look through the Contents page and chapter headings as you will rarely have to read a book from cover to cover. If it is an article or chapter, read the introductory and concluding paragraphs to get an idea of the main points being covered.
- Once you have discovered how a piece is structured, you will be better able to follow an argument and distinguish between the main ideas and examples. So, read the section you are interested in twice. Firstly, read it through to get the general meaning, then read it again more slowly, concentrating on the points you did not quite understand during your first attempt.
- When we learn, we assimilate new information by associating it with something we already know. If the topic is new to you, you can help make connections between what you are reading and what you already know if you jot down any questions you have – what you want to learn from a passage – before you start.

G.E. Sutcliffe[1] has likened this to shopping. Normally, you make out a shopping list and go to the places which will have what you want. If you are not quite sure what you are looking for, you go window shopping first.

So, when you read, you need to go through the following steps:

- *Purpose.* Consider why you need to read the material. It is possible you need to read the entire book to critically evaluate the views of the author. It is more usual that you will want to add to written material that you have already obtained, or want to collect material for an assignment. Look first at the course syllabus and any notes that you already have.

- *Questions*. Write down the questions you have. You will recall the saying that unless you know where you are going, you will not know when you have got there. The same applies to reading and learning.
- *Read*. Use the Contents pages, sub-headings and indexes to home in on the sections you want. Read and underline, or make notes of key points depending on your purpose.
- *Review*. Check whether your questions were answered, and if not consider where you need to look for the answers.

Note-making

You will need to make notes for a variety of reasons, including taking notes from lectures, talks and seminars, and making notes for assignments and revision. Note-taking is different from note-making, and we will deal with taking notes in lectures in the next section. Here we look at making notes from a book or article for assignments, references or revision.

Good notes are notes which remind you of the connections you made at the time of writing, to concepts you are already familiar with. It is best to 'translate' ideas and concepts into your own language. Your own notes will be more use to you because it is easier to recognise and remember your own patterns of thought than to rely on handouts or rewriting other people's ideas. Pages and pages of neat notes which paraphrase the work of different authors on a topic are not good notes, as they merely add more information and in effect you have sets of notes, rather than one set of notes.

Good notes are clearly structured, contain key points, and are presented in a manner which makes it easy to extract information when it is required. For that reason, note-making is very personal, and other people's notes never seem to make as much sense as your own!

When you are making notes from books or articles, you should follow these guidelines:

- *Put the ideas into your own words*. Putting other people's ideas into your own words will help you remember them and your notes will be more useful to draw on for assignments. If you do copy out material, for example, quotations, make sure that you note the reference details. If you accidentally use the material without remembering where it came from, you could be accused of plagiarism, which has very serious consequences.

- *Use key points.* Make notes in the form of key points. It will waste time during revision if your notes are too detailed. Use headings from the book you are using in case you need to check for extra detail at a later time.
- *Organise your notes.* A different file for each major subject of the course is highly desirable, with file dividers so you can subdivide the information into topics. Colour coding makes retrieval more easy and more interesting. Pages should be numbered, and as you collect extra information to add to your file you can draw up a subject index. Notes from books you have read and any other supporting material, such as handouts, can be conveniently filed next to lecture notes, so providing a comprehensive source of information which is more manageable when time comes for revision.

Active Listening

Listening effectively is essential to effective study if you are to learn from lectures, videos and tapes or group discussions. This section is called Active Listening because listening should be active as opposed to passive. Listening is different from hearing, which is much more normal, 'in one ear and out of the other'. Unfortunately, students often switch off because talks are poorly structured or their mind has wandered elsewhere. Because we make connection with other experiences or knowledge, one of the very techniques which helps us to learn also hinders our listening. What often happens is that you make a connection with another situation or example, and when your concentration returns to the talk, the point has moved on. However, you can usually catch up if the lecture is well structured and visual aids are used.

Active listening involves filtering and selecting information, concentrating on particular words and phrases, and associating what is being said with what you already know. There are three main situations when you will be required to listen carefully and the following tips will help you listen effectively.

Listening at lectures or meetings

On most IPM courses you will be given lectures. Even on a Flexible Learning course there will be opportunities to attend a lecture or talk given by an expert. You are likely to be encouraged to attend meetings of your nearest IPM branch where a lecture may last around an hour, and this time span is hard to cope with. A real danger with lectures and talks is to switch off early on because you think the topic or speaker will be boring and of no interest. You will not be able to concentrate at the same level throughout a talk and you will have to take steps to counter the loss of concentration.

There are six rules for keeping yourself alert during talks:

1. Anticipate

When listening, look ahead and try and anticipate what is coming next. Consider why are you being told this. Try to link what is being said with your own knowledge of the subject. Put yourself in a critical frame of mind and react to what is being said, either agreeing or disagreeing with the concepts. If you have been able to do some background work on the topic before you arrive, this will be of help.

2. Listen for key points

Listen for key ideas or concepts being presented and distinguish between ideas and illustrations, examples or anecdotes. Do not expect a lot of major themes. It is more likely that a speaker will cover one or two main themes and a few subsidiary points.

The majority of speakers add personal comments and examples, even jokes, as they deliver a lecture. Your task is to identify the main themes and note these, leaving out supporting material unless it seems valuable. If everything seems valuable, ask for a handout so that time can be spent discussing points.

3. Look for signals

Normally a speaker or lecturer will indicate when they are coming to an important point as they will say so or maybe they will highlight the point on the flip chart. These are some of the signals to look out for:

- Phrases to introduce new ideas:
    A major development . . .
    Here are two reasons why . . .
    And most importantly . . .
    First . . ., second . . ., third . . .
- When introducing supporting material, these phrases may be used:
    On the other hand . . .
    In contrast . . .
    As an example . . .
    Furthermore . . .
- A summary/conclusion could be indicated by:
    Therefore . . .
    From this we can deduce . . .
    To sum up . . .
    Finally . . .
- Some lecturers will give very clear signals about things they consider important with phrases like:
    The important thing is . . .
    The basic argument is . . .
    Remember that . . .

4. Be active

Many students think that attending a lecture is a passive activity where the tutor does all the work and the student merely listens and takes notes. Regrettably, many sessions are like this and rapidly become monotonous for both tutors and students.

Most speakers will look to the audience to see their reactions and will respond if they are interested and alert. Whether you are interested, puzzled or bored will be shown by your facial expression and body language. If you want to get the best out of a speaker, show you are interested in what is being said by looking directly at the speaker and use facial gestures such as smiles or nods of understanding.

5. Ask questions

Form questions in your mind and jot down those which you could use at the end of the talk. Asking questions is important to ensure you have understood what the speaker has said and it will also communicate to your lecturer what concepts there may be difficulties with.

6. Take notes

Taking notes is important because it focuses your mind on the main ideas, and helps you to store points on paper for future reference.

You should never take notes as if taking dictation. Writing down everything that is said means you have little chance to absorb the full meaning of the talk, and make any connections to your own knowledge and experience. It is, however, possible to write quickly, putting down most of what is said in your personal 'shorthand type' scribble. Although such notes won't make perfect sense at the time, you can sort them out after the lecture and write them up neatly and coherently. This helps you digest the material, and is useful for learning, especially if complemented by further reading and study.

It is beneficial to jot down your own reactions or examples which you think of which will illustrate the points the lecturer is making. If you put these in the margin, or in a different colour, they can be useful to come back to later, and may be helpful for future assignments.

There are several different methods of taking notes and we will examine these later in this chapter.

Listening to tapes or video recordings

To help with your studies it is always worth taping relevant radio or TV programmes. For useful examples and case studies in say the Corporate Environment or Employee Relations modules, or for up-to-date information on Employment Law and national training, you should scan the TV and radio listings for relevant documentaries or discussion programmes. VCR is particularly useful as most students find that greater concentration is required for listening to cassette tapes. We rely on the non-verbal clues given to us by a speaker, so listening without visual clues is more tiring. Therefore you may find that you have to work in shorter time spans.

The important points in listening to tapes are:

- Listen to the tape without taking notes first of all in order to get an overall picture.
- Read through any notes provided with the tape.
- Listen to the tape again and pick out key phrases and themes, taking notes.
- If the topic is difficult to grasp, stop the recording so you can go back over your notes and consolidate what you have heard.

Listening in tutorials and group discussions

As indicated earlier, small group discussions will be a regular feature of your course, but many students find it difficult to learn from them. Sometimes it is difficult to follow and take part in the discussion because you hear points or arguments with which you disagree. Alternatively, there may be people who 'hog the limelight', interrupt other group members, and try to force through their own point of view. In a tutorial, difficult people will be handled by the tutor, but in a self-help study group, you may have to do some negotiating if all participants are to benefit from listening to each other.

To help you learn from group discussions or tutorials, make notes, paraphrasing the content of an important point. If available, use a flipchart so that everyone can see their ideas being summarised, classified and used as a springboard for further exploration of the topic.

Methods of Recording Notes

There are several different methods of recording notes and you should choose the method which is most appropriate for your

needs. Here we will deal with the two most commonly used
methods.

Linear notes

This is the most obvious method because we read and write in
linear form, but there are a number of ways of making linear notes
more useful:

- *Layout*. Visual impact is important both for clarity and memory,
  so notes should be divided into headings and sub-headings. Key
  words and ideas should stand out well so that you can see, at a
  glance, the main points and overall structure of the topic. One
  approach is to divide the page into two columns, putting the
  main points on the left hand side and supporting details on the
  right hand column.
- *Ordering and emphasis*. Use numbers, roman numerals, letters
  and brackets to indicate main and subsidiary points and underline all headings that need emphasis.
- *Colour*. Colour can be usefully used to distinguish key points or
  underline important headings.
- *Abbreviations*. Evolve your own way of abbreviating common
  words, but make sure you always use the same ones! Abbreviations such as 'mgt' or 'trg' can be used to save writing out these
  common words.
- *References*. Always note the sources you are using, including the
  page number. It can be frustrating when writing an assignment if
  you have to go back over a book or article to search for an
  important passage. Your sources will of course need to be
  indicated in the Bibliography at the end of assignments.

Pattern notes

Pattern notes, or mind maps or webs as they are sometimes
known, place the main heading in the centre of the page and then
subheadings and key points radiate respectively from the centre
and subheadings. Key words and phrases are used, with words
usually printed. Colour coding and arrows are used to connect
ideas. Drawings are often used to illustrate points.

:]]]]]

]]]]]

An illustration of pattern notes is given below for the topic of listening.

Pattern notes have some advantages over linear notes. The relationship between the various aspects of the topic become more obvious and you should be able to see a topic from different angles. This can be an advantage when planning reports or assignments or preparing to give short talks.

If you want to experiment with pattern note-taking, you should consult Tony Buzan's book *Use your Head*, BBC Publications, 1975.

References

1. SUTCLIFFE, G.E. *Effective Learning for Effective Management*, 1988.

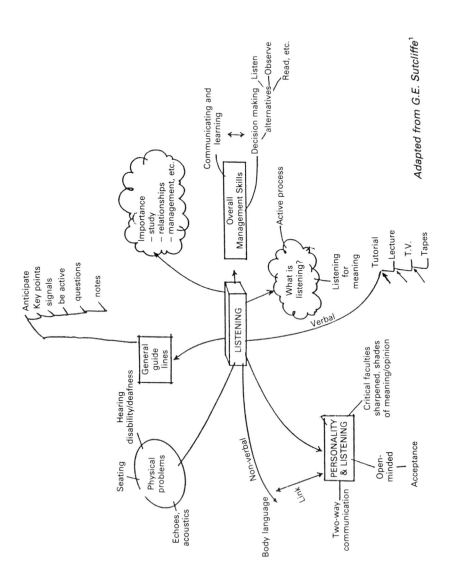

Adapted from *G.E. Sutcliffe*[1]

Chapter 5
The management report

All centres running IPM courses are responsible for assessing their own students' assignments and management report. Guidelines are provided to course tutors on the methods of assessment to use, and the assignments and management report are monitored by IPM appointed examiners to ensure that standards are maintained. This chapter will explain how to undertake a successful management report and the next chapter will cover assignments, as the basic formula of the report can be adapted to them.

Purpose of the Management Report

The management report is completed towards the end of the programme as it gives you the opportunity to bring together and apply your learning from the course and demonstrate your professional competence. It is a requirement that a 'live' human resource management issue or problem is investigated, and data collected and analysed, so that conclusions and recommendations to management can be made. It will therefore involve a detailed study in your own organisation or an organisation with which arrangements have been made for you to undertake the management report. The demands of the management report are considerable and we will look at choosing an appropriate topic, how to go about investigating it, and how to write it up in an appropriate format. The flowchart on the next page outlines the sequence of activities in preparing your management report. First of all, we deal with selecting an appropriate topic.

Choice of Topic

In most cases, you will be expected to decide on the topic yourself and agree it with your employer and college staff. The majority of

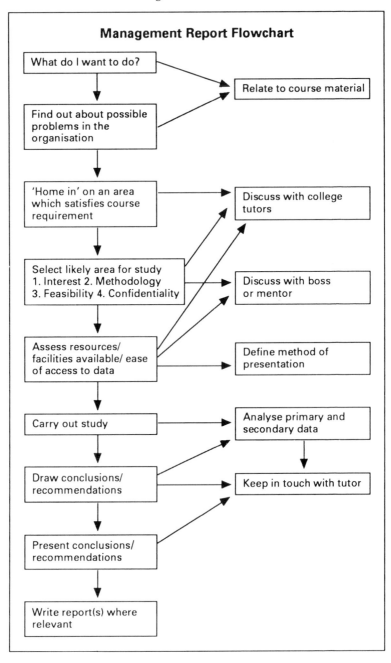

Management Report Flowchart

What do I want to do?

Relate to course material

Find out about possible problems in the organisation

'Home in' on an area which satisfies course requirement

Discuss with college tutors

Select likely area for study
1. Interest 2. Methodology
3. Feasibility 4. Confidentiality

Discuss with boss or mentor

Assess resources/ facilities available/ ease of access to data

Define method of presentation

Carry out study

Analyse primary and secondary data

Draw conclusions/ recommendations

Keep in touch with tutor

Present conclusions/ recommendations

Write report(s) where relevant

IPM students are on their study programme with the knowledge, and hopefully support, of their immediate boss, and therefore there should be an understanding from the start of the course that a management report is to be undertaken. This may mean that your boss already has some ideas on a suitable topic, which may or may not be an advantage to you! However, assuming you have a reasonably free choice, there are a number of factors that should help you decide on a suitable issue or problem to investigate.

Interest

Perhaps the most important consideration is that the topic is of interest to you and to your organisation. You will be putting a considerable amount of time and effort into the management report and if your interest is not high you are not likely to have the motivation to do well. Similarly, if your organisation does not have any interest in the findings of your investigation, it is less likely to provide you with the support you need. You should therefore choose a topic which you do not mind 'living with' for the length of time concerned.

Opportunity

The management report is intended to give you the opportunity to demonstrate that you:

- understand the principles underpinning the topic
- have considered alternative approaches to investigating and analysing an issue
- have obtained primary and secondary data and generated alternative solutions to the problem or issue
- have taken a critical, evaluative approach enabling you to draw relevant conclusions
- have considered the feasibility of introducing your recommendations into the organisation and prepared an implementation plan
- can write a report and present data in a clear, logical way with appropriate charts and diagrams.

Therefore, you need to choose a topic which is going to enable you to demonstrate all these abilities. If, for example, your employer suggests that you draw up an induction programme for new starters, you will have a hard task to do something original which will be broad and deep enough in scope to gain a good mark.

On the other hand, if you suggest that you review the effectiveness of the recruitment and selection procedures as a whole, or communication systems in the organisation, this will give you much more scope. You would need to take a critical view of what constituted effectiveness for the organisation and would have to undertake an investigation involving line managers and employees, as well as consider the large body of academic literature on these topics. You could draw on all three subjects in the Stage 2 syllabus, and you would be able to consider the feasibility of introducing your recommendations into the organisation and produce a plan for implementation.

Your employer may take the view that any practical project for the benefit of the organisation should be acceptable. You will need to make it clear that there are educational objectives to be met, and try to come to a mutually acceptable topic.

Your course tutor will be able to give you advice as to whether a topic will be sufficiently demanding and original. Gaining the positive support and encouragement of your tutor for the topic you have chosen can be a great boost to your morale and may pay dividends. Discussions will generate new dimensions for you to explore. So, remember that it is much harder to do an excellent management report on a poor topic than a poor report on an excellent topic. Make sure that you choose a topic which gives you the opportunity to do well.

Time

Completing an investigation and writing up a report always takes longer than you think. Often you will meet unexpected obstacles or the topic of the investigation may turn out to be too ambitious. Some comments taken from the self-assessment sheets of students who recently completed their management report are worth passing on.

In answering the question 'What changes would you make if you were to carry out a similar investigation?' one individual wrote '. . . complete the research before starting to compile the report.'

Another admitted in answer to the same question 'I would take the oft imparted advice of . . . and various tutors along the way and start the whole project very much sooner.'

The importance of clear terms of reference but, at the same time the need to cope with the unexpected, was a message frequently repeated.

> It requires single minded commitment and clarity of mind to bring the process to a satisfactory conclusion. Perhaps the most difficult task is to define the parameters of the report and keep them in mind whilst remaining flexible enough to adapt to new information and events as they present themselves.

> It was very easy to become side-tracked into associated issues which were not stictly relevant to the purpose of the investigation. Getting clear objectives is an important stage in the process. At the same time, however, it is necessary to remain flexible, to the extent that unexpected information may come out of the investigation, which needs to be included in the report.

There are a number of points therefore to bear in mind in managing your time with the management report. First, start to identify a problem or issue worthy of the management report very early in your study of Stage 2. All activities will take time and need to be scheduled properly. Work back from the deadline for submission and set key time horizons. Allow extra time in case things do not go to plan.

Secondly, bear in mind that late submission of your management report will hold up your graduating from the course. Although the actual amount of time for completion is determined by individual colleges, the results must be sent to IPM House one month before the exams in order to be taken into consideration.

The figure opposite shows the approximate allocation of time for the major stages of your management report.

Resources

As well as checking that it will be possible to complete the management report within the allotted time, you also need to

Stages	Approximate proportion of time
Arranging project Choice of topic Agreement of issue with host organisation	$\frac{1}{5}$
Preparatory study Methods of investigation Preliminary study of organisation Pilot study Literature search commences	$\frac{1}{5}$
Main investigation Collection of primary and secondary data	$\frac{1}{5}$

Evaluation
 	
Testing of models and concepts
    against evidence
Drawing implications
Forming conclusions and
    recommendations
	$\frac{1}{5}$

Report Drafting the sections of the report Editing Typing, proof-reading and binding	$\frac{1}{5}$

Adapted from Adamson[1]

make sure that any resources you require will be available. These include covering your costs in travel and phone calls, information searches, postage and photocopying. If you need information which may be restricted, you will need to check that access will be permitted, as much as possible, without incurring additional costs, such as writing software to get at the data! Finally, you need to arrange for the management report to be typed or word-processed (if you are not planning to do this for yourself), proof-read and bound.

These arrangements may pose difficulties for the student who is not working in personnel, or does not have the support of their organisation. Again, the difficulties are shown from the comments on one student's self-assessment sheet:

> My offer to undertake a training needs analysis was refused as the Department Head did not consider any kind of training needs analysis necessary. After several attempts to identify a project which the department would accept, I gave up completely and decided to work on my own at home, getting the information I needed as best I could. This was done mainly through a network of acquaintances and colleagues in other organisations.

Hopefully, the Continuous Professional Development initiatives of the IPM will encourage more personnel staff to take responsibility for assisting in this area and to treat mentoring as an essential part of their own personal development.

However, there will be some students who face totally unanticipated difficulties, such as a job change or being made redundant, which affect the resources available for their project. If there is a risk of such events happening to you, choose a topic where data sources already exist and you can draw upon them within a timescale to suit your own requirements. It is also possible that some students may be working in an environment where a suitable topic cannot be identified. In such cases, individuals should discuss alternative ways of completing the management report with their course tutor as early as possible. It may be that an alternative can be arranged such as:

- undertaking an investigation in a host organisation known to the college or within the local IPM branch. For example, an evaluation of a management development programme.
- producing a report which tackles a general issue and uses other students on the course as the source of data. For example, an

unemployed part-time student considered child care facilities for working mothers and undertook an investigation of the policies and arrangements of five local employers.
- producing a report drawing as much as possible on the student's knowledge of their organisation, but utilising secondary rather than primary data to justify their findings and conclusions. For example, if the organisation were to introduce performance-related pay, what are the problems and issues which might arise?

Other examples of topics which might lend themselves to a management report include the following:

- Employee Resourcing:
  - –the analysis, over time, of the results of the implementation of an equal opportunities policy
  - –the strategic use of part-time employees and an analysis of the terms and conditions which could/should be offered
  - –the analysis of how far current compensation packages contribute to reaching business objectives.
- Employee Development:
  - –the development and implementation of an appraisal scheme for management staff
  - –the identification of needs for multi-skilled training and flexibility, and preparation of training programmes
  - –the use of mentoring in training strategy.
- Employee Relations:
  - –the planning for, and introduction of, harmonised terms and conditions in your work place
  - –the analysis of an industrial dispute within your workplace and the development of a strategy to reduce the chance of a similar problem in the future
  - –an analysis of the implications of, and the need for, a new technology agreement and the design and implementation of such an agreement.

Once you have identified a possible topic or issue for your management report, you should consult your tutors in order to check whether it will be suitable.

Identifying the Problem

At this stage, you will need to define precisely what the problem or issue is that you will be investigating. For example, you may decide to investigate absenteeism as everyone says this is a problem in your organisation. You will need to talk to key people, e.g. personnel and line managers, and probably a sample of employees or their representatives to clarify the nature of the problem. For the topic of absenteeism you would want to ask: Is the problem substantiated by statistics on absence rates? Is there a problem in comparison with other organisations? Is absenteeism just a symptom of a wider range of causes? What are the consequences of absenteeism for other employees? What operational problems are caused, e.g. in work scheduling or holiday cover? What are the costs?

By working your way through this process of questioning, you will get down to identifying the real problem. What seemed like an absence problem may turn out to be poor job design or bad management/employee relations. Or relating the problem to other organisations may reveal that flexible working systems are used elsewhere, and your investigation may need to evaluate the costs and benefits of introducing such a system.

Once you have gone through this analysis, you will be able to define and agree your terms of reference. For example for the topic of absenteeism:

The aim of this project is:

a) to investigate the causes and consequences of absenteeism in the manufacturing division of XYZ company; and
b) to recommend a future strategy for the effective management and control of absence.

You will now have most of the notes you need for the introductory section of your report, including:

- *Problem description.* The background to the problem, its context and significance.

- *Terms of reference*. The purpose of the report, its scope and limitations and what it is intended to achieve.

You will also have ideas on the next section of the report, the methodology:

- possible methods of investigation and timescales
- what information will be required, how it will be obtained, and the analysis which needs to be done.

Obviously, you may find later that you have missed out on an important factor and have to redefine the issue. But if you think through the questions which the topic poses at the start, you will have a clear focus for your investigation.

You will now be ready to submit a short synopsis, usually called the project proposal, for formal approval. The project proposal will normally include the following information:

- *Short title*. A working title which can be refined as the investigation proceeds, and changed if you decide to pursue a different avenue.
- *What the report is about*. A paragraph or two explaining what the topic involves in order for an appropriate subject supervisor to be allocated.
- *Why there is a problem*. An explanation of why the problem is worthy of investigation and indicating the hypotheses to be tested.
- *Methodology*. An outline of the intended methods to be used, e.g. interviews, questionnaires, for discussion with your project tutor to ensure that they are appropriate and feasible in the context of the problem outlined.
- *Support*. A description of the degree of support that can be expected from your employer or other people in the organisation where you are conducting the investigation.
- *Difficulties*. Possible problems which might arise in conducting the investigation and your thoughts on how these could be tackled.
- *Time schedule*. An outline timetable for the various stages of the work, which can be modified later if needed.
- *Confidentiality*. An indication of the extent of confidentiality

which might be required for the management report when produced.

Conducting Your Investigation

Once you have identified a suitable issue or problem to investigate and got your course tutor's approval for your project proposal, you have to get down to the hard bit – conducting your investigation. A number of questions will have come to mind. What does 'methodology' mean, and what is the difference between primary and secondary data? A review of the literature sounds very 'academic' – how will you go about this? What support can you expect from your college tutors? And how do you organise yourself? This section will deal with these questions, and first of all we start with recording systematically the information you collect.

Recording information

Before you start to collect data for your management report it is wise to think through what will be the most appropriate method of recording the information you gather. A notebook will be needed to jot down ideas and information as you come across them, and for making notes when interviewing or consulting people. A system of loose-leaf file paper or index cards will be useful for quotations, summaries of material and for preparing a bibliography.

Whenever you make use of source material you should record the following details carefully and systematically:

- author's name
- title of book, article or document
- date of publication, place and name of publisher
- page numbers

There is nothing more frustrating and time-consuming than to remember later in your project that you came across something highly relevant but you have no record of it.

For opinions of people consulted, the name, job title and organisation, date of interview, place of work and telephone number should be recorded. If you are interviewing people you will need to record your findings carefully for future use. If it is possible, take tape recordings to back up your notes, but ask for permission first, and check interview summaries with the people you interviewed to make sure you correctly understood the opinions being put forward.

You could also refer back now to Chapter 4 and remind yourself of the key points about reading and note-making, as they will also be relevant to your work for the management report.

Tutorial support

A member of staff from the institution at which you are studying should be appointed to supervise you as you prepare your report. Normally the topic you choose to study will determine who is appointed. So, your tutor for Employee Relations will be likely to supervise projects which fall into that syllabus, although if another member of staff is recognised as having a particular interest or expertise in say, job design and new technology, they would take over a project in that area.

Staff resources are usually such that it is not possible for students to choose a favourite tutor as their supervisor. It is however helpful if you can strike up a good relationship with a tutor who has an interest in your topic area, and would be available to give you support.

Your project supervisor will give you guidance on how to approach your investigation and should be able to direct you to reading and sources of information you have not considered. As the project progresses, the supervisor can help considerably as a sounding board against which to try out your ideas, and will ask you questions that will require you to justify your ideas and conclusions.

The IPM indicates to colleges that seven hours' tutorial support for students should be provided for the preparation of the management report. This can cover a range of activities, such as:

- examination of 'the problem' to identify the various components
- advice on appropriate methodology
- guidance on sources of information
- advice on methods of presentation
- reading of drafts of the report.

Sometimes tutors will bring together students working on similar topics to share ideas and progress in an 'action learning' type of activity, but more often you will meet on a one-to-one basis.

The onus is upon the student to make contact and arrange appointments with their supervisor at regular intervals. Occasionally students will decide to work alone and not consult their supervisor, but experience shows that students who do so tend to misunderstand what is required of the management report and can fail. Also, you should be aware that your supervisor will probably be involved in assessment of the report and will be consulted by other assessors as to the amount of effort you put into the project. So, for example, the assessors would want to be aware of any student who investigated a very original topic on which there was little written material and for which a great deal of primary data had to be collected. It will also be taken into account if a student has had to produce a report without the support or encouragement of their employing organisation.

Methodology

Your choice of appropriate methods to use to collect information will be an important decision. You should check out with your project supervisor whether the methods you propose to use will be feasible for the problem and context you are investigating.

You will, of course, have to find out details about your employing organisation in order to provide background information about the context to the problem. You will also have to decide whether researching other organisations will serve any purpose, and what information from external sources is needed.

In order to gain people's views and opinions, individual or group interviews should be undertaken, or you could decide to administer questionnaires. You will need to choose an appropriately sized sample, taking into account the likely response rates. As well as gaining official approval to approach the sample population, it will be necessary to think through how to approach people and explain the purpose of your research, and to set up a procedure for distributing and collecting questionnaires. Confidentiality is an issue to be addressed.

It is important to be flexible in the amount of time you allocate for collecting information. Inevitably, reminders have to be sent out to people to return questionnaires, and setting up interviews can take time and lead to delays if key people are called away to deal with more urgent and important matters.

Review of the literature

A literature search is one method of gathering information that all students are expected to undertake. Showing that you understand the principles underpinning your chosen topic is an element of assessment of your management report, so you need to find out about the academic theories and concepts and known 'best practice' in your field of study, even if there is very little written on the topic.

Sources of information will include textbooks and journal articles, reports of similar investigations, and the media. You should seek the advice and assistance of the subject librarian in your college, as they are usually only too happy to help in tracing sources, and often comment that IPM students do not use them enough. Your college librarian should be able to provide bibliographies and booklists, and many libraries are linked up with computerised data-banks. The IPM Library and Information Service has a list of bibliographies for popular topics, and reading lists can be prepared on special request.

The management report is not an academic thesis, so you are not expected to consult hundreds or even tens of books. On the other hand, you are expected to read more widely than the essential textbooks and to make use of some special sources in your area of investigation. Clearly this will vary according to the topic: if you are doing a report on an aspect of equal opportunities, for example, the problem may be deciding what not to read. The important point is to consult relevant and up-to-date sources that can inform your investigation and show that you are familiar with the principal authors on your area of study.

No matter what the outcome of your literature search, it should always be described in the methodology section of your written report.

Types of data

We indicated above that you will need to consider both primary and secondary data. Primary data is that which you collect yourself by direct observation, interview, questionnaire, or other means. It has the advantage that you can tailor your information-gathering to your particular requirements. However, it tends to be a time-consuming process and considerable skill is required to draw up well-designed questionnaires or interview checklists. This is certainly an area where your project supervisor can help.

Secondary data is any information that has been collected by others, and it includes company statistics or records, results of surveys or government sources of statistics. The advantage of using secondary data is that you can rapidly access a wide range of information. However, it may not have been gathered for the same purposes as your own study and will therefore have limitations. From your study of Management Information Systems you should be aware that it is possible to lie with statistics!

Pilot study

You should design your methods provisionally and try them out on a selected sample to see if they are appropriate. This 'pilot study' will show up people's misinterpretation of questions asked in questionnaires or interviews. It will reveal any difficulties in recording and analysing data. For example, if you decide to tape your interviews but do not have access to an audio typist, it could take many more hours than anticipated to play back, note and summarise the statements made by the interviewees, and you may amend your approach after your first sample.

Some form of pilot study should always be included. Unfortunately, many students launch with enthusiasm into their investigation without a pilot study and then find that there are snags which either cannot be rectified or result in loss of valuable time in going back to the beginning.

Evaluation

As you proceed to assemble relevant academic concepts and examples of best practice, and obtain data on the problem or issue you are investigating, you will be weighing up one against the other. You will begin to build up your own 'model' or 'hypothesis' which will be modified and improved as your investigation progresses and you gather more information.

You may have collected views or theories which you feel are not particularly useful for evaluating the data collected. In which case, discard them. As this is a report to aid management decision-making, not an academic thesis, do not be tempted to pad out your report with material which is not pertinent or with background which is only incidental to the main theme.

You should find that, as you relate your chosen theories or concepts to the information you have collected about the problem or issue, you will begin to draw out implications in terms of patterns, trends and forecasts for the future. You will now be ready to start writing up your management report, and we deal with the usual layout of reports in the next section.

As an example of where you should have got to, we take the topic of absenteeism which was used as an illustration on page 55.

Conducting an Investigation into Absenteeism

Organisational background

1. What policies/procedures are there to control absence and what solutions are there?
2. How is absence monitored?
3. What training has been given to managers/supervisors on absence management?
4. Have there been any previous studies/reports on absenteeism in the organisation/industry?

Methodology

1. Primary data
   –Information on absence and its causes from questionnaires and/or interviews with personnel and line managers and hopefully employees and their representatives.
2. Secondary data
   –Statistics on absenteeism and attendance records, looking

for frequency and duration of absence, any seasonal or departmental variation or prevalence among particular employee groups.
–Statistics from other organisations belonging to the same parent company or other companies.
3. Literature search
–Articles and studies of practice e.g. *Employment Gazette* or IDS publications.
–Writings on the causes and control of absenteeism.
–Academic theories, e.g. Herzberg

The Structure of Your Management Report

Some institutions specify their requirements for the layout of reports, and you would be wise to check for any particular conventions where you are studying. However, the following aspects are normally required in the order shown:

1. Title page
2. Acknowledgements
3. Contents
4. Summary
5. Introduction
6. Methods
7. Main body divided into chapters or sections
8. Conclusions
9. Recommendations
10. Bibliography
11. Appendices
12. Glossary

Title page

This should show the title, subtitle if any, the date, author's name plus position and organisation if appropriate. The qualification for which you are studying should also be shown at the foot of the page. The title should be concise and arouse interest while clearly indicating the subject matter. Do not overcrowd the page: a clear, simple layout is by far the most attractive.

Acknowledgements

The acknowledgements page enables the author to express thanks to those who have helped with the project and should give their name, job title and organisation. This is only a matter of courtesy but it lets the assessor see how successful you have been in persuading others to lend their interest and support.

Contents

It is important to set out clearly the main chapters or sections, and sub-sections if necessary, giving their page numbers. It should give sufficient detail to enable the assessor and other readers to easily locate any particular aspect to which they wish to refer. The table of contents should also list appendices, major figures, diagrams, illustrations, etc. if applicable.

Summary

This is sometimes called an 'abstract' or the 'executive summary' because it enables busy people to get the gist of the report without having to read it all. It should follow the contents page and be no longer than one page in length. The summary will simply state the objective of the report, the main methods used and summarise the conclusion and recommendations as briefly as possible. Do not back up these points with facts or arguments – these come later.

Introduction

Although the format and content of the introduction will vary from report to report, it provides an opportunity to make readers aware of the background information and aims of the report.

- *Background.* Include information about the organisation to enable the reader to grasp the circumstances of the report. The amount of detail will depend on the knowledge of the readers. For example, if you are working for a large public sector organisation very much in the news, you can take it for granted that certain background facts will be known by the reader. If, on the other hand, your organisation is less well known you will need to provide enough detail to place the issue in context, such as sales turnover, number of employees, culture and management style, sophistication of personnel policies and procedures.

- *The issue.* The problem or issue with which the report is concerned should be identified. If you are seeking a solution to a problem, you should indicate how the problem came to light and the scope of the investigation. If you have chosen a particular issue to examine, say why, and by whom, you have been asked to look at this issue. Any constraints inhibiting your work could be briefly mentioned.
- *Terms of reference.* The objectives of the investigation should be clearly stated so that the reader knows precisely what the report is about.

Methods

This section explains how you went about the investigation, for example:

a pilot study was undertaken . . .
interviews were conducted with . . .
questionnaires were sent to . . .
XYZ documents were examined . . .
observation checks were made at . . .

The aim is to show the reader the thoroughness with which you undertook the investigation. If particular obstacles were encountered which prevented you from making some enquiries, these should be stated so that the assessors know why you did not explore that area.

Main body

The main body of the report is made up of major sections or chapters, with subheadings and numbered points. For example, if

you are writing a report on systems of working hours, one of the
areas under investigation may be flexible working hours, and your
work might take the following form:

1   Flexible working hours
1.1   Principles of flexible working hours systems
1.1.1 Core time
1.1.2 Flexible time
1.2   Attitudes of Departmental Managers
1.2.1 Favourable responses

. . . and so on.

In planning these sections, follow a clear, logical order. One
approach is to outline the concepts and theories which relate to the
topic, then the evidence found and finally your evaluation.
Alternatively, a series of sections could each deal with one set of
concepts, the evidence and evaluation.

For example, if you are writing a report on appraisal systems,
the sections might be as follows with the first approach:

1. Theories and best practice on appraisal.
2. Appraisal systems and procedures in the organisation.
3. Evaulation of (2) compared with (1) to reach conclusions.

And with the second approach:

1. The appraisal system in the organisation compared with
   theories/best practice.
2. Appraisal procedures and processes evaluated for effectiveness.
3. Communication and training arrangements in the organisation
   reviewed in the light of 'best practice'.

The latter approach is more demanding because it requires the
integration of theoretical and practical information to pull out the
implications of your findings. But it makes for a more interesting
read and is the more managerial approach. Students often adopt
the first approach because they find it easier to paraphrase and
summarise the information they have found from reading, before

going on to analyse and discuss what is happening in their organisation.

It is up to you to decide the best structure, but you should ensure that you have:

* included the theoretical and practical information you have gathered
* analysed, assessed and discussed future options with arguments for and against each
* arrived at conclusions about what should be done.

It is not sufficient merely to throw a lot of information at your reader and not do any analysis. You know more about the subject of the investigation than your reader, so you should say what you think should be done. Your line of argument should be clear so that the assessors can see why and how you have come to your conclusions.

The text should be kept concise and the argument should flow smoothly. Some details can be put in appendices, but it is important that all essential information is in the body. The reader should not have to refer to the appendices in order to understand the body. A reference to an appendix should say, for example:

The detailed statistics on labour turnover are contained in Appendix 2, however in summary these show . . .

or

The application form was examined for objectivity and it was decided to amend certain sections. The original application form and the form as amended are to be found in Appendices 5 and 6 respectively.

Do not forget to consider the financial implications of any courses of action you are putting forward. Your recommendations for change may be modified in the light of a cost-benefit analysis. The Chief Examiner who looks at management reports commented that many were lacking in this area but that those which did address financial issues were likely to be (rightly) awarded the highest marks.

Conclusions

The conclusions draw out the main points of your report and present a considered judgement on them. No new material should be contained in the conclusions. For example, you should not quote the names of academic sources which have not been previously used to analyse and interpret the information in the main body.

If the previous parts have been clearly and logically constructed, the conclusions will flow naturally from them, maintaining your line of argument. In summary, the conclusions should state:

- the nature of the situation or problem
- the likely consequences if it continues
- what can be done, possible courses of action, and their costs and benefits.

If necessary, reference by page number and paragraph can be made to a point in the body of the report.

Recommendations

Sometimes a report may end at the conclusions, leaving others to decide on the appropriate course of action, but recommendations are normally required to put forward your proposals as to how the problems identified should be overcome. The following points should be borne in mind:

- Recommendations should be set out in sentences, which may be numbered for ease of reference.
- They must be related to a problem which is discussed in the body of the report. One student recommended a complete managerial restructure 'to improve communication', when nothing had been mentioned in the report about this being a problem!
- State concisely what should be done to resolve the issue or problem.
- Recommendations must be feasible, and the reader should be able to see how they could be put into practice.

- You should be able to justify why you have made these recommendations.
- State clearly any implications of the course(s) of action, changes, etc that you have proposed.

References and bibliography

You will need to indicate the sources you consulted as a basis for the report and may want to suggest others as further reading. Make clear what you are providing. If you want to include items which might be of interest to the reader, but to which no direct reference has been made, the list is normally called a bibliography. This would list all of the reading done in preparation for the report, and show authors' name, title, data and publisher. You may make reference to documents produced within your own organisation, course handouts, books or articles you have consulted.

References should normally include only those sources which have been directly referred to in your report. They can be either listed in the order they appear in the text, in which case they should be numbered, or included at the end of your report as an alphabetical list. Whichever system you use, you must make sure that the text ties up directly with the reference source quoted.

Appendices

This is where you put the detailed additional information that supports your findings. Graphs, charts, plans, calculations and company information are often put in the appendices. But remember, if a chart or graph is directly related to the text, it should be included in the main body of the report. For example, if you were writing a report on the effect of inflation on employee relations strategy, a table showing changes in the retail price index would be included in the body of the report. If your report was about employee relations policies in your organisation, the table would probably be better placed in an appendix.

Glossary

A glossary can be of help if your report refers to technical or specialist terms and some of your readers are not familiar with them. If it is very specialist language, it is best to define any technical terms as you go along.

Writing up Your Report

One of the greatest difficulties for anyone is actually drafting the report. You will have assembled a lot of material and have some idea of the structure but putting it all together in a coherent way demands a great deal of effort. The best way of organising yourself is to:

- Set out, on one very large piece of paper, the main sections you propose to use in the report.
- Put each major heading on one sheet of A4 and fill in the main sub-headings, key points and tables, figures and associated appendices.
- Check this against the structure proposed in the previous section, to ensure that the sequence is right.
- Write out a draft for each section or chapter.
    - It doesn't matter where you start. It can help focus your thoughts if you write your conclusions first. At any rate, do not feel you have to start with the introduction and slog through to the end!
- Consult your college supervisor.
    - Legible handwritten papers can be discussed with your supervisor. It is best to seek advice at this stage, when it is easier to make modifications and rearrange parts and maybe do some rewriting.
- Write up the complete report and have it typed for a final discussion with your supervisor.
- A report should be bound along the left-hand margin for ease of reading and have covers stiff enough to protect it from any rough handling in the post.

The IPM guidelines are that the report should not exceed 7,000 words, excluding appendices, and a report which is much longer than this will not usually be welcomed. Most tutors and managers would argue that an essential skill is the ability to produce a concise report within the limits set and an appropriate length will be a factor in assessment.

Style

The style of writing should be factual and objective. You should not allow prejudices or emotional responses to intrude into your report. There will be some biases which creep in, but the main thing is to be aware of your biases towards, for example, people you interviewed whom you got on well with. As you write, keep checking back to your terms of reference so that you stay on track.

An important convention when writing reports is the use of the 'impersonal construction' which basically means that you avoid using 'I' or 'we'. So, for example, instead of writing 'I found that . . .', you would write 'It was evident that . . .' or 'The statistics revealed that . . .' And instead of writing 'He said . . .', you would write 'It was reported that . . .' or 'Respondents indicated that . . .' But, while too many 'I's can grate, 'the author' sounds very formal, and can be equally off-putting.

At the same time, it should be apparent what your level of involvement and contribution has been. In reports which carry the impersonal construction to the extreme, the nature of the authors' contribution is not always obvious. You want to make it clear what is your own work and ideas as this is what you are being assessed on. So, it is best to check with your college supervisor to see what style of language is preferred.

Writing English

Students frequently gain fewer marks than they might because their use of English is inadequate. Sometimes they write in such a way that their meaning is unclear and the assessor fails to realise what they are trying to say. In other cases, grammatical and spelling errors are serious enough to incur penalties.

Try to use short sentences and short words and your meaning will be clearer. A useful check for clarity on these two aspects is the 'fog index'. An index of over 12 is considered to indicate a heavy or difficult piece of writing. Newspapers and magazines are usually lower, probably around 10 or less. To calculate the fog index, the procedure is as follows:

Take a short passage of text (approx 100 words). Count the total or words in the passage and divide this by the number of sentences to give the average number of words per sentence. Count the number of words of three or more syllables and add this to the previous total. Finally multiply by 0.4 to give the fog index.

For example, the following paragraph has 78 words in five sentences and a fog index of 11.8.

Similarly you should avoid over-long paragraphs. Ideally a paragraph should be between 75 and 100 words long and, more importantly, it should relate to a single topic or idea. If paragraphs are too short your writing will seem disjointed. If they are too long, the text can seem dense and forbidding and your reader may find it hard going. Paragraphs should be linked so that the first sentence of a new paragraph links back to the previous paragraph.

To get a feel for what the finished article should look like, it can be helpful to see examples of reports other students have written. The actual content will not be particularly useful as each report is unique, considering a specific situation in a particular organisation, and your tutors are not looking for a standard approach. However, sometimes they will run a session which gives the whole group the opportunity to look at previously prepared reports. If not, check whether you can gain access to completed reports. In some institutions, a copy of students' project reports must be given to the library as a permanent record.

We have assumed here that your management report will be produced in a typewritten format. If you want to be more innovative, you should discuss your ideas with you tutor first, so as to ensure that the assessment system can accommodate alternative forms of presentation.

Assessment

The responsibility for assessing both the management report and your assignments lies with the centre running your programme. It is considered important that tutors who have knowledge of students and their individual circumstances should have discretion in marking. The IPM provides guidance on marking bands, and these are shown in Appendix C (page 74). As well as the internal assessor(s), colleges are required to appoint an external examiner, or moderator, who is approved by the IPM, to monitor the standards of the reports and assignments.

The marks given to each student report must be recorded on a pro forma. The sample marking sheet provided by the IPM is included as Appendix D (page 76). Your college may have a different form; an example from one centre is shown on page 78. This college example has five dimensions and five levels of performance. An evaluation of performance is made and the appropriate cell is ticked. Each grade is then multiplied by the weighting factor to produce a mark for that dimension and all the marks are totalled.

EXAMPLE: A project which is excellent in identifying the problem, good on methodology, weak on analysis/use of literature, but has fair conclusions/recommendations and presentation would receive the following marks:

Identifying the problem	5 × 5 = 25
Methodology	4 × 3 = 12
Analysis/Literature	2 × 5 = 10
Conclusions/Recommendations	3 × 5 = 15
Presentation	3 × 2 = 6
Total	**68**

References

1. ADAMSON, A. *A Student's Guide to Assignments, Projects, Field Studies and Research*, 1986

Appendix C
IPM marking bands

Assignments/management report: 70% or more

The work achieves the objectives set; demonstrates comprehensive understanding of the material; applies relevant knowledge to questions asked/skills examined; shows the ability to exercise judgement; incorporates some originality; excellent presentation; a comprehensive piece of work which overall achieves a very high standard.

Assignments/management report: 60–69%

The work achieves the objectives set; demonstrates a broad understanding of the material; applies relevant knowledge to questions asked/skills examined; shows the ability to exercise judgement; incorporates some originality in evaluating the problem but lacks the originality and depth of judgement of the top band; on the whole the presentation is very good and the overall standard above average.

Assignments/management report: 50–59%

Achieves only an adequate coverage of objectives; demonstrates an understanding of the material but is somewhat simplistic in the application of knowledge to the question/skill; lacks any depth of evaluation of the issues; shows some imprecision in arguing or presenting the case and may be 'woolly' in parts; overall, however, it achieves it objectives and what it lacks in some areas is compensated for in others.

Assignments/management report: 49% or less

Achieves an inadequate coverage of the objectives; shows some basic understanding of the material but tends to contain errors or go off at a tangent and is descriptive rather than evaluative; argues and presents the question/task poorly and does not achieve an adequate standard.

Appendix D

Sample IPM marking sheet

MANAGEMENT REPORT – STAGE TWO

MARKING SHEET

Name of student:

Full title of project:

Date project handed in by student:

Name of First Reader:

Name of Second Reader:

Date by which the marked project should be returned to the Project Director:

CRITERIA	MAXIMUM MARKS	MARKS GIVEN

TOPIC AND PLANNING

Clarity of definition; method of approach and investigation as compared with possible alternatives; application of course learning.

TREATMENT AND PRESENTATION

Extent, methodical examination and appropriateness of source material; quantity and quality of data produced; effective collation and ordering of material; conciseness and clarity, relevant use of graphs, charts etc.

FINDINGS AND CONCLUSIONS OR RECOMMENDATIONS

Relevance and soundness in relation
to the information and analysis
produced; logicality; practicability;
cohesiveness.

TUTORIAL DISCRETION – First Readers should build marks
into the first three categories where compensation is
required under the following elements:

Background to the production of the
project (including job or domestic
changes), effort in relation to capacity,
source availability and difficulty of the
subject; degree of support from the
students organisation (where
appropriate); learning achieved.

_____ _____

_____ _____

Any additional comments:

Date: Signed

Sample College Marking Sheet

Project Assessment Sheet	EXCELLENT 5	GOOD 4	FAIR 3	WEAK – REFER 2	FAIL 1	WEIGHTING FACTOR	MARK
Identification of problem						5	
Methodology						3	
Analysis and use of literature						5	
Conclusions and Recommendation						5	
Presentation						2	

STUDENT................   DATE SUBMITTED...................

TUTOR.................   DATE MARKED...................

COMMENT.................

TOTAL =====

Chapter 6

Assignments

Assignments on your IPM courses will very often involve writing a report of about 2,500 words. They are very useful practice for the preparation of the management report. The format outlined in the previous chapter may be too formal for assignments; however, the structure will be a useful guide. A simpler format is likely to be appropriate, as follows:

Title page
Introduction
Body
Conclusions and possibly recommendations
Appendices if required
Bibliography

Page numbering is also a good idea.

The IPM requires that all assignments should incorporate the development of skills drawn from the syllabus. This means that your assignments will often be work-based and will involve a wider range of skills than traditional essays. To get the information you need, you will have to exercise your face-to-face communication and influencing skills. Both theoretical knowledge and practical ideas will have to be drawn on to produce creative solutions. You will usually need to adopt the perspective of someone more senior than yourself in the organisation. The objective is to demonstrate not only that you know what you have been taught, but that you know how and why to apply it and can tackle problems with a managerial focus. Otherwise, students would gain high marks for simply copying out relevant answers to questions. There are some specific points about doing assignments as distinct from undertaking the management report.

1. Clarify what is required.

Before starting, be clear about what is being asked of you. Establish the scope and limitations of the task and the method of presentation before you start to write. As well as reports, you may be asked to produce work in a variety of formats, including:

  memos
  letters
  advertisements and press releases
  training manuals and instruction leaflets
  personal diary

Each of the above will require a different layout and use of language.

2. Think about themes.

Assignments will usually be intended to develop and test you in some aspects of the course material you have already covered. So you can start by jotting down some notes about what you already know and understand about the subject, and possible themes. You may have ideas which will eventually be rejected, but this process will help you to begin to structure the assignment in a coherent manner. Also, at this point, you will begin to realise the gaps in your knowledge and once you know what is wanted, you can start filling in the gaps. Pattern notes are particularly useful for this stage of assignment preparation.

3. Read your notes.

Go back over the notes you have made earlier in the course to see if anything is relevant. From the point of view of learning, this has the added advantage of assisting your memory as you review and recall earlier material. If you have been wise, you will also have newspaper clippings, articles and references already filed away, which can be consulted.

4. Background reading.

You will probably have to do some background reading. Books and articles which are relevant will usually be on the reading list supplied by your tutor, but you may need to consult the library catalogue for additional or more specific reading material.

Now is the time to use the guidance on reading and notemaking given in the earlier chapter. Also, do not forget to consult fellow students and work colleagues for their ideas.

5. Plan the structure.

Now you can go on to planning the structure of your written assignment in the same way as we outlined for the management report. A tip to remember is that it is much easier to write a good paragraph which fits into a well-ordered scheme than it is to embark on a 2,500-word piece with only a vague idea where it is leading. So, time spent dividing the work into clear stages and units really pays off when you come to do your writing. Plan each section in detail, and always keep in mind the topic you are addressing.

6. Refer to management literature.

Use academic concepts and theories where appropriate as many of the marks for assignments will be allocated to how you incorporate these. Your course is intended to equip you with a set of conceptual tools and techniques which can be applied to a variety of situations. So, even if you have been set a work-based assignment, it is expected that you will draw on particularly relevant theories, concepts and examples of best practice. Initially, this may feel strange, but by the end of your course, it should have become second nature.

You should avoid padding your work with long descriptions of standard issues in organisational and management literature, for example, Maslow's hierarchy of needs. You should just ensure that you have included the central points and made reference to the source. Do not plagiarise, but present your own views, or make it clear when you are stating someone else's view.

Quotations can lend interest if kept short. If you use direct quotations you must either:

- put in a footnote with a precise reference to the source of that quotation
- give a brief reference linked to a bibliography at the end.

But you do not want too many acknowledged quotations. Only use those phrases which are so telling that no paraphrase of the author's idea will be as effective.

Techniques to ease the process of writing include the following:

- use one side of paper and leave blank lines to insert new ideas
- cut and paste paragraphs into sequence (or use a word-processor)
- picture your audience and keep your objective in mind, which is to persuade the reader
- provide a 'controlled release' of information with each paragraph dealing with one principal point and leading to relevant conclusions.

Writing Essays

Sometimes you may be given an assignment which asks you to discuss or evaluate a concept or idea in terms of its usefulness or effectiveness, perhaps in your organisation. The assignment question could be phrased like the following examples:

---

1. *Evaluate the case for prohibiting the use of the injunction procedure in industrial disputes.*

2. *Discuss the view that the purpose of employee relations is to resolve the conflict over the price of labour.*

3. *How, if at all, has the concept of human resources management altered personnel management?*

4. *What are the most common problems with performance appraisal schemes, and how can they be overcome?*

> 5. *Outline your organisation's induction training arrangements and explain how you would set about improving these arrangements.*
>
> 6. *Discuss the use of computer-based training in education and training.*

A list of the types of instructions you are most likely to be given for assignment essay work and tips for tackling them is given in Appendix E (page 90).

A common fault with assignments of this type is for students to write all they know about the topic and then be puzzled when they get a low mark. The reason for this is not that they know too little, but that they did not do what the question asked them to do.

To illustrate this, consider your reaction if you asked someone 'Which bus goes to the town centre?' and they proceeded to tell you all they know about buses. You might be impressed by their knowledge, but not consider the information relevant. Similarly, your tutors might be impressed by what you wrote but not be able to award high marks because the information was not relevant and had not demonstrated your ability to relate what you have learnt to the specific question.

So, how can you tackle assignments like this and get it right?

Examine the wording

When you are given an essay title, take it down exactly and examine the precise wording to see what is being asked of you. Does the question or title call for a general treatment or for specific cases to be illustrated, a broad outline or a detailed account? Are you expected to state your own personal experience and opinions, or simply to demonstrate your knowledge of other people's? Are you asked to refer to any particular source of data? Are you expected to describe things as they are (or were) or analyse and explain why they came to be that way? Need you discuss implications and suggest applications?

So, for example, with the questions illustrated above, the wording indicates you should:

1. Give the case for and against using injunction procedures, making reference to examples of (recent) industrial disputes,

and give your own appraisal of the case for making a change in the legal framework of the employee relations system.

2. Examine the argument being put forward; define your understanding of the view which is stated, and give the strengths and weaknesses of this position with supporting examples, leading to a balanced conclusion.

3. Like question 2 above, this question requires you to define your understanding of the concepts and give arguments for and against, with examples, leading to a balanced conclusion.

4. Indicate the main problems you are aware of, but do not go into a lengthy description of examples and their causes. Concentrate on tackling the second part of the question and provide guidelines on how the problems can be overcome in future.

5. As with question 4, this asks you to indicate the main aspects of induction, but does not demand a detailed explanation of induction in your organisation. Indicate which aspects you would improve in the future and how this could be done.

6. As with all questions which include concepts, you would need to define your understanding of the term then, in this case, go on to consider the strengths and weaknesses, with examples, leading to a balanced conclusion.

Think about questions

In the chapter on reading and note-making, we said that to get results you must read purposefully, with a set of specific questions that you want answered. Your essay title is too broad and it needs to be broken down before you can begin any useful research. The best way to do this is to ask yourself questions about it. These questions will then guide your reading.

EXAMPLE:

Suppose you are asked to *Discuss the use of computer-based training in education and industrial training.* You might begin to analyse the title and come up with a set of questions like these:

---

1. What is computer-based training (CBT)? How long has it been in use?

2. Who uses CBT most, and why?

3. Is CBT used in similar ways in education and in industrial training, or differently?

4. How does CBT compare with other forms of learning? What sort of results does it get? What do trainees think of it? Are there any difficulties attached to using it?

5. Will it be used more or less in the future? Will it be used in new ways? Will other, newer methods take its place?

As you read you may come up with other questions, and some of your original thoughts may be less relevant, but the more clearly you know what information you are looking for, the more easily you will find it.

Write an outline

The next step in planning your essay is to work out the basic structure or outline. Doing this has several advantages:

• It helps you sort out what are the main ideas and the important details.
• It makes sure you leave out nothing vital and that you do not repeat yourself.
• It allows you, once started, to write fluently without having to keep chewing your pen and wondering what to say next!

The following framework will be useful for a wide variety of essays:

1. Introduction

• Comment on subject of essay. What do you understand by it? How is it important? Give any essential definitions.
• Outline which aspects you will deal with and why. Signpost the sequence of material which follows.

Do not summarise the main arguments – save this for the conclusion.

2. *The main body*

- Develop your line of argument through three or four main ideas.
- Support each main idea with examples and illustrations drawn from personal experience or other authors.

There will often be two different points of view and three to four aspects of a topic. In most of the example questions given above there are two contrasting points of view, and certainly several aspects which can be covered. So, at the very least you should be able to produce six or eight paragraphs. You can organise your material using a matrix pattern, as illustrated below.

EXAMPLES: Using a matrix to organise your material

For the question, *Discuss the use of computer-based training in education and industrial training*, we have already identified that we should consider the strengths and weaknesses of CBT. In addition, there are several aspects which we identified when we analysed the title and produced a set of questions (above), such as (a) current use of CBT, (b) comparison of CBT with other forms of learning, and (c) possible uses in the future. The matrix would look like this:

	Argument	
Analysis	**View 1** **Strengths**	**View 2** **Weaknesses**
Aspect A Current use of CBT		
Aspect B Comparison of CBT with other forms of learning		
Aspect C Possible uses of CBT in the future		

You can now decide the most appropriate sequence for writing up the answer. Sequence A takes each aspect of the first view, then each aspect of the other view. Sequence B considers the strengths and weaknesses of each aspect in turn. The topic and your personal preference will probably help you decide the best sequence, but sequence B is likely to make more interesting and lively reading.

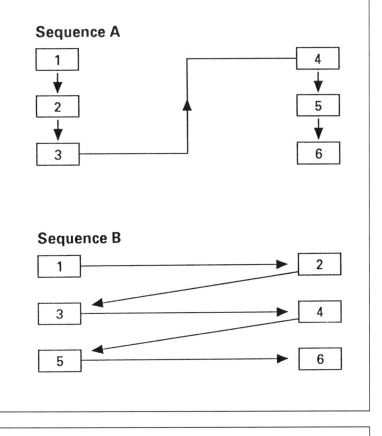

Another exampe of this approach is illustrated by the question, *How effective is the structure and style of the personnel function in assisting your organisation to meet its objectives? What adjustments could be made in order to render this function even more effective?*

Aspects	Argument	
	Strengths	**Weaknesses**
A. Present structure of personnel management responsibilities		
B. Style of handling personnel issues		
C. Possible adjustments for the future		

For the question, *Discuss the case for the closure of un-economic pits in the coal industry*, the matrix could look like this:

Factors	Argument		
	Stakeholders		
	Government	**Employees**	**Consumers**
A. Economic			
B. Social			
C. Political			

With the types of structure shown in the boxes, and an introduction and conclusion, your essay can be produced. As you plan your outline, a rough guide to the length of each section is:

Introduction	8%	of the total length
Body	76%	of the total length
Conclusion	12%	of the total length

3. Conclusion

- Sum up main ideas and arguments.
- Give an answer to the question.
- Indicate wider implications or future trends, or scope for further consideration.

It must be clearly stated what the conclusions are and why they have been reached. You do not have to be 'for' or 'against' something in your conclusions. You may decide, after considering the evidence, that you cannot make a judgement because the evidence is inconclusive. This is perfectly valid, as long as you say why.

Avoid limp repetition of earlier ideas and phrases in the conclusion. It is often best to write the conclusion first because:

- It gives a sense of direction to your writing if you know exactly what conclusion you're heading towards.
- It helps ensure that your essay will conclude firmly and definitely, rather than just stopping lamely as so many do.

Write the essay

You should now be ready to write your essay without any difficulty. There are a few final points worth bearing in mind when writing assignments:

- Use a clear structure which follows the pattern of the question where appropriate. Refer to concepts and key words in the question, as you write.
- Present your work with clear paragraphs and headings. Concepts should be clearly defined or outlined with reference to their source and their application should be demonstrated.
- Use interim summaries to show how far you have proceeded in your discussion or evaluation, and include signposts to let the reader know what to expect.
- Use clear, jargon-free expressions. If you do have to use unusual terms, a short glossary may be required.
- Use diagrams, numerical data and charts, as 'a picture conveys a thousand words' and they don't usually count towards a constrained word count for answers.

Appendix E
Essay questions

Analyse   Study, identify and describe the main characteristics in depth.

Assess   Make a judgement on the strengths and weaknesses of the arguments for and against something.

Comment   State your views on something, supporting them with evidence or explanations.

Compare   Emphasise similarities but do not forget to mention differences.

Contrast   Emphasise differences but do not neglect to mention similarities.

Criticise   Make a judgement about the merit of the statement. Be specific and give the results of your scrutiny.

Describe   Outline the main features in an ordered way.

Discuss   Examine the strengths and weaknesses of particular arguments and give a balanced conclusion.

Evaluate   Appraise the material, stating strengths and limitations.

Explain   Clarify something, looking at the causes and major features.

Outline   Indicate which are the main aspects and how they relate to each other.

Chapter 7

Case studies

What is a Case Study?

Case studies are scenarios of typical situations you are likely to face in real life. They range from mini-cases of one to two pages in length to full-length cases of 30 pages or more. In the examinations you will be presented with mini-case studies, while in assignments you could be given either type of case study.

The majority of case studies describe real situations, as perceived by the case writer, but sometimes cases will be constructed or modified to emphasise the teaching and learning points upon which your tutor or examiner wishes to focus. Frequently case studies contain a series of things which have gone wrong because good management practice has not been followed.

Why Are Case Studies Used?

A well-prepared case study provides an excellent way of testing your understanding of concepts and theories, and your ability to apply them to practical situations. We said in the previous chapter that you may be given assignments which ask you to use examples from your own experience. Case studies complement this type of assignment and are often used as a form of assessment for students who have less work experience.

As a personnel manager you would be involved in investigating situations, identifying the root cause of a problem, and then advising on ways to solve the problem, or making recommendations for change. So, the objective of case studies is to get you to apply the theories and concepts that you have learned on the course to the scenarios presented.

For example, if you have been studying motivation theory and management style, you may analyse a case study in which you find that one manager treats employees with respect and encourages them to improve, while another treats employees like machines. In your written work, you could briefly describe McGregor's theory X and Y and illustrate how the managers in the case exhibit the characteristics of Theory X and Theory Y managers. So the value of case studies is that they enable you to demonstrate your competence in applying your learning and your skills in problem-solving.

How to Approach Case Studies

As with all other activities or assignments, the exact approach will depend on what you are being asked to do in the assignment or examination. However, the following guidelines can usually be adopted:

1. Read the instructions

To ensure you understand what you are being asked to do!

2. Read the case study

Read it once or twice to get a feel for the main components, such as the setting, key players, and obvious problems or examples of good or bad management practices.

3. Identify the main issues

Look for the key problems or issues facing the case study organisation. Try to look beyond the obvious to see if some apparent problems are merely symptoms of more deeply-seated ones. For example, low morale may be symptomatic of poor management practice, lack of involvement or ineffective communication; conflict frequently arises from conflicting objectives and overlapping responsibilities.

Look for links between problems because organisational problems are often interrelated. Use key concepts you have learned on your course to provide a framework for your analysis, and make use of techniques such as calculating key ratios, to enable you to make more sense of any figures provided.

4. Develop a solution

Once you have decided on the problem areas to be addressed, you can think about the options which could be followed. Here again, you will be drawing on course concepts to suggest better ways of operating.

You may find that you have to make certain assumptions because data is not provided in the case study. For example, in considering recruitment methods, the options will vary depending on whether the economy is booming or in recession, and hence whether there is low or high unemployment. In your write up, you should state clearly any assumptions you do make, but you should not add anything which materially affects the content of the case study.

If you feel that there is a lack of some specific data, you should indicate the sorts of areas you would want to investigate further in reality, to cover all aspects fully. In the example above on recruitment methods, you may feel that data on staff turnover is relevant and you should indicate how this information would have helped you.

Once the options have been identified, you will then need to evaluate them. Forecast their likely effect on the problem or issue and on the organisation as a whole, and then reach a set of conclusions and recommendations for dealing with the situation. Depending on the given task, you may also be required to think through how you would implement your plans. This would entail identifying any constraints or obstacles, for example, time available or cost implications.

5. Plan your answer

Unless instructed otherwise, you should present your answer in an appropriate report format covering all or some of the following, depending on what the question asks you to do:

1. Introduction and background.
2. Statement of problem(s) or issue(s).
3. Effect of the problem/issue(s).
4. Factors causing them.
5. Possible solutions and implications.

6. Conclusions and recommendations.
7. Appendices and supporting evidence.

After preparing your plan, re-read the case study and questions and check that you have included everything which was required.

6. Write up your answer

In writing up your answer, you should try to show that you have thoroughly understood the problem(s) and applied course concepts to an analysis and interpretation of the information provided. Conclusions and recommendations should be realistic in the context of the case study and real life; they should be both practical and feasible in the light of the circumstances in the case and any constraints. Furthermore, you should seek to show that you have taken into account all relevant information in the case, and your conclusions and recommendations are logical and consistent.

These general guidelines will be useful whenever you are given a case study to work on; however, the mini-cases which you face in the examinations will place extra demands upon you. For a start, there is the time factor. You will have some reading time, but steps 3 to 6 above will have to be completed within 45 minutes or less. You will not be able to refer to your textbooks or notes for course concepts which may indicate solutions to the problems identified. You will be required to bring together your learning across a range of topics or disciplines and recommend sensible and practical ways forward. We will therefore now look at how to handle a case study question in the Stage 2 examinations.

Tackling the Case Study Exam Question

A feature of the examination papers at Stage 2 is the compulsory integrated question, which is usually in the form of a case study. The objective of this question is to examine students on the core programme in the three subjects of Employee Resourcing, Relations and Development. It is intended to assess whether you have integrated your learning over these three core areas and can demonstrate that you understand how the various facets of personnel management relate to each other.

The Chief Examiners will check the following features in assessing an answer:

- The answer must be based on the case study material.
- Students must integrate what they know about particular subjects raised in the case study, rather than writing their answer as if from three different perspectives.
- An understanding of the case, the issues raised and their interrelationships must be shown.
- The written answer must be presented as a coherent analysis and discussion.
- The answer includes a plan of action based on the issue(s) raised by the question.
- An appreciation of the implications of the proposed strategy and plan of action is shown.

All elements of the syllabuses can feature in the compulsory question, so it is not possible to 'question spot' by looking at past exam papers. The question will always require problem resolution from the viewpoint of a personnel practitioner who understands how the three subject areas of personnel management can be applied to a personnel problem or issue. Always try to look at the problem from several different angles, and if you have relevant work experience, bring this in to add strength to your answers. A comment from the examiner's report on Employee Resourcing in the summer of 1991 indicates that the objective of the question is to see how you would handle difficulties, not how you would avoid them!

> Some produced answers that showed an unwillingness or inability to tackle the difficulty and presented instead very general exhortations about how to turn a 'bad' business into a 'good' one, with chunks of academic discussions about motivation, culture and social responsibility. These answers generally failed.

In the IPM Stage 2 examinations, equal weight is given to all four questions, including the compulsory question. But it does have a special importance as examiners are directed to note particularly the quality of the answer to this question when reviewing marginal candidates. Although it is not essential that the integrated compulsory question is passed in order to pass the paper as a whole, it is expected that candidates will normally pass it. Therefore, it is sensible to make a special effort on the question, and to take it first, rather than last. Since there is 10 minutes' reading time before the start of the exam, you can use this effectively by reading and re-reading the case and beginning to think through the main issues and possible solutions.

Example of compulsory question

You and your personnel colleagues have audited the personnel activities throughout the organisation and have produced the following list of issues requiring attention in the next twelve months:

a) The scheme of performance-related pay that you introduced six months ago has been heavily criticised by other managers because of it being tightly controlled by the personnel department. The Chief Executive complains that the pay bill has increased by 17%, although you estimated an increase of 8%. There has been an increase in union membership attributable to the performance pay scheme, with assertions that it is divisive and unfair. There is a union claim that it should be discontinued, with the existing level of pay increase redistributed equally between all employees.

b) Modifications to the middle management development programme to fit within the Management Charter Initiative (MCI) framework of management competences has been criticised by senior managers as not being sufficiently geared to the needs of the organisation, although many of those taking the programme feel that this element improves their general career prospects.

c) The Chief Executive was recently invited to address a meeting of the local Rotary Club. Several other members of the organisation were in the audience and reported the following extract from the address:

> 'I think our Personnel Department is pretty useless, but in my experience they always are.'

---

d) The introduction and development of a new computer-ised personnel management information service has improved the workings of the personnel function, provid-ing extensive and rapid data that was not previously available. You are convinced that this has enhanced the credibility of personnel in all parts of the organisation – no matter what the Chief Executive may have said.

Your personnel colleagues have asked you to draft an action plan to tackle these four issues. What will your draft plan contain?
(Note: It is permissible to make assumptions by adding to the case details given above, provided the essence of the case study is neither changed nor undermined in any way by what is added.)

The box question is taken from the Employee Resourcing examination, May 1992. In the case there are four issues to tackle and the guidelines indicate that it is permissible to make assumptions by adding to the case details given. However, it is not wise to over-interpret this invitation, as some students did – and removed all the problematic features of the situation!

So, having made sure that you first of all base your answer on the case study, the next step is to look for the interrelationships between the issues. There is a clear indication that the personnel department has lost credibility and the confidence of organisation members. Performance related pay (PRP) is being criticised by both managers and union representatives. The management devel-opment programme is being criticised by senior managers, and the Chief Executive is reported to have said the personnel department is useless. The perception of the personnel function is therefore that it is ineffective. However, from the point of view of those working in the personnel function a major step forward has been taken with the introduction of a computerised personnel manage-ment information service (CPIS).

Moving on to exploring the issues raised, you can take both the general issue of effectiveness and reputation of the personnel function and the specific issues of PRP and management develop-ment. Some questions come to mind, like: 'How is the personnel function organised at present?', 'Are the roles of personnel specialists advisory, administrative or executive?', 'Is the personnel department represented in senior management decision-making?' You could make some assumptions about these aspects, but it would be far better to recommend to your personnel colleagues that a further audit is undertaken to examine the needs of the organisation and to compare them with the personnel function that is provided.

It will be necessary in your answer to indicate that you have some understanding of the issues raised. In the May 1992 exam, many students seemed not to be aware of the MCI framework, and those that did often took an uncritical view of it. They should have brought in their knowledge of this aspect of the Employee Development syllabus by indicating briefly why an MCI competence framework is beneficial and why it is difficult to implement in practice.

Similarly, with the issue of PRP, you need to write briefly about both the benefits and difficulties of this approach to remuneration. There is a phrase in the case which indicates managers are blaming the personnel department for the problems. You can point out the tendency for managers to grade all their staff as 'above average', and consider whether there are flaws in the scheme, lack of suitable appraisal training, or whether the location of budgetary responsibility should be reviewed.

There is of course a link to the CPIS. We can read in the case that there is now extensive and rapid data available which was not previously. Perhaps the benefits are not being taken up by line managers because they are not aware of the potential of the system.

Overall, the analysis of the issues and diagnosis of the problem(s) should show that you understand the relationships between the problems or issues covered by the case. But you must now go on to produce a draft plan for tackling the issues. The question quite clearly states that this is what is required. Regrettably in May 1992, many students were able to produce quite a good diagnosis, but were not able to go on and produce a draft plan, and were therefore not likely to get a satisfactory mark for the question. Included in the plan would be practical measures to modify the opinion of the Chief Executive, address the problems being experienced with PRP and the MCI competence framework, make the personnel department more responsive and effective and 'sell' it to its customers.

All of the above points would of course be thought out before you start writing. You would produce a plan of your answer using the format for case study answers provided earlier in this chapter. This would ensure that when you write you present an answer which is coherent, and focused on the issues raised, and provides a plan of action for dealing with the situation. Which is of course, what the Chief Examiner is looking for!

Chapter 8

Revision techniques

Often the thought of revision can be much more daunting than the act. What makes revision so daunting is the prospect of having to revise all you have learnt on the course. It is thinking about the amount of work which makes it frightening. To overcome this, a 'plan of campaign' in relation to revision and exam preparation should be worked out at the start of your course. And, if you have followed the guidelines in previous chapters, you will have already made significant inroads into the task, in that you have:

1. a filing system
2. sorted your notes into topics
3. written your notes in a structured and easy-to-follow way
4. reviewed your work as you progressed
5. obtained copies of syllabuses, past exam papers and examiners' reports on each examination.

Even if you are not this organised, all is not lost. This chapter will cover the revision techniques that you can introduce into your personal study plan, as well as the assistance you can expect your tutors to provide. Also, it is likely that you have previously sat and passed exams, so cast your mind back to the techniques which you found useful then. Other students will have their own tips on revision techniques, and books like this can be consulted to add to the help you get from your tutors.

If you are reading this chapter at the start of your studies, well done! Revision should be a continual process, starting in the first week of your course. By going over your work constantly, reading through your notes, amending and improving them as your knowledge increases, and looking over textbooks and other materials, you will find that things begin to make sense, and will transfer from your short-term into your long-term memory, ready to be recalled during the examination. Of course, you will still need to go over in some depth the topics you are to be examined on, but if you have managed to review your material throughout the course, the final revision period will be more effective, and not the burden it might be otherwise.

Getting Going on Your Revision

You will probably need to start your revision about four to six weeks before the examinations. In the same way as you prepared a personal study plan, so now a revision plan is required, and you will probably find you use your time more effectively if you go through the following stages.

Information on examination

If you are entering for the IPM's national exams, there is one examination per subject, and a standard format with 10 questions. Many universities have been approved to set internally assessed exams and they won't necessarily follow the IPM's model. Therefore, if you haven't done so already, you should now obtain past exam papers and analyse these for the sorts of topics covered and the type of questions asked. Look at the format of the paper and how many questions there are to choose from.

As we said in the previous chapter, the IPM Stage 2 national exams have a compulsory integrated first question on each of the three papers, and many internally assessed centres have adopted a similar format. Other centres have exams based around case studies which are issued in advance of the exam to allow prior preparation. In some cases there may be an open-book exam, allowing students to take into the exam any case materials or notes they have prepared. You should therefore check what is allowed to be taken into the exam at the institution where you are studying.

Question spotting

Many students try to identify from an analysis of past papers those questions which are likely to appear. This is not recommended as past trends are not reliable predictors in exams. However, with a little research, it should be possible to identify those areas of the course which are central and must be learned, those which look useful and those which look less important. There are also bound to be some areas of the syllabus which you find particularly interesting, maybe because you have personal experience, and others which you find more difficult. You therefore have to make a decision on how best to devote your time and energy.

It is dangerous to limit your revision only to the number of questions you have to answer, and you should not bank on particular topics coming up. However, there is an advantage in selecting some topics so you can concentrate your work and go into greater depth of revision.

Topics

When you start your revision, it will seem as though you are faced with a vast volume of information, and your first task will be to reduce this as much as possible. Organise your material into topic areas, using the major divisions of the syllabus for each exam.

The word 'topic' should be interpreted in a broad way. For example, in the Employee Resourcing syllabus, Recruitment and Selection is a topic, which can be broken down into sub-areas such as psychological testing, interviewing, recruiting across national boundaries, etc. So you might categorise Recruitment and Selection as central to personnel management and well worth revising, but it would not be wise to limit your revision to one of the sub-areas. You need to revise the whole topic of Recruitment and Selection so that you have plenty of scope for flexibility in answering questions.

In making a selection of topics, look for overlaps of knowledge between various areas of the syllabus and even between different exams. For example, for the Stage 2 Employee Resourcing exam, you may revise termination of employment, discipline and disciplinary interviewing. You will find that this will help you in revising for the parallel exam in Employee Relations in which termination and disciplinary issues are also part of the syllabus.

Similarly, revising the topic of appraisal schemes for Employee Resourcing will help you revise for Employee Development.

Thus, you should not compartmentalise your revision scheme into work for each exam, but consider it as a total work package. Only in this way will you be prepared for the compulsory integrated first question on each of the national exam papers.

The process of identifying overlaps will be assisted if you revise all your subjects in parallel, as you will be able to spot the common areas and begin to see your revision as a process of integration. Often many students will say that it was only just before the exams that something clicked and all the pieces of the jigsaw puzzle fell into place. It is better late than never, but if they had been reviewing their material consistently throughout the course, these connections would probably have enlightened them earlier!

Your course tutors will also be able to give you advice on the topics it is worth concentrating on and the level of knowledge which is needed. For example, in Employee Development, it is not necessary to learn the details of legislation on employment and training, but you should know broadly what are the principal features of government intervention over the last 25–30 years. However, your tutors can only indicate their opinion of current key issues and topics, and have no crystal ball which enables them to see the exam questions which the Chief Examiners have set. Therefore you should revise as widely and comprehensively as you can.

If your analysis of the exam paper indicates that 10 topic areas are regularly assessed, and you have to answer four questions, it would be reasonable to revise six areas as your preferred topics and two as your reserves. Even if you can answer every question, the examiner will never know this as you are only required to answer four. However, if you are happier revising the whole syllabus, this is what you should do, as it is best to adopt the method which suits you best.

Revision plan

Once you are clear about the exam requirements and which topics you are going to revise, you need to design a revision plan. Some students may be forced into cramming in the day or two before the exam, but for most students, cramming only makes for confusion and stress. Assuming you have allowed yourself several weeks for revision, a plan is the key to working effectively. This is similar to the study planner which we suggested for use at the start of your course. When you have worked out how much time you have available, you should write down what you intend to cover in each session. To do this, you will need to think about the topics that need revising and put them in some sort of order.

There is a natural tendency for students to revise the easiest and most enjoyable subjects first, but you should tackle the most difficult topics first. Otherwise you might keep putting them off and never actually get around to them! If you can cover the most difficult topics first, this will give you a sense of achievement and confidence and the going will get easier all the way.

When you have gone through all your material and made extensive lists, work backwards from the exam dates, and make sure you can fit in all the topics in the time available. The subject revision table shown on page 109 could be used for each examination, but remember to prepare an overall revision plan. As we said above, you should revise your subjects in parallel, and not compartmentalise your learning.

It is not always necessary to have long stretches of time, but try to use the odd half hour before a meal, or while travelling to work. And remember to allow time for contingencies – perhaps a week for any delays or set-backs, or for final preparation. Also allow time for practising past exam papers. Tick off each piece of work completed on your revision timetable, as this will help your motivation. Leave time on the day before the exam for running through the main points of the subject and for getting an overall perspective.

Revision Strategy

As you start your detailed revision, you will have a mass of information. You will have notes from lectures and background reading in loose-leaf files which will be the basic material for your revision. A second source of material is past assignments and projects which you should read again to see if you have changed or deepened your understanding of the material and whether you have taken on board your tutor's comments. Also do not forget to review what you learned in skills development activities, as you can make reference to them in the exam – for example, the problems encountered with panel interviews in a class exercise.

Reduction of data

Condensing your original notes progressively is an excellent way of absorbing material. Most students find that doing something practical is better than merely reading material over and over again. You should therefore go through your notes and write out the key points on a blank sheet of paper. In this way you will concentrate the information and reduce the volume. As the exam approaches, you should go over these notes again and progressively reduce them. As a result, some students find that they can end up with their revision notes for each topic on one sheet of A4 paper or on a small index card by the time of the exam. This process should provide you with a set of key words to learn and at the same time has helped you memorise the information. For an example of the progressive reduction of data, you should consult Michael Pitfield's book in which a chapter is progressively reduced to one page of key words.[1]

You will still probably have to learn a limited number of things using rote learning but index cards can be particularly helpful here as they are so portable and you can learn from them in spare moments when your brain is not otherwise occupied. You can also take them with you as you set off for the exam and if you have some time while waiting and start to feel nervous, you can glance at your revision cards. Once you get into the exam, you will find that your key words form the framework for your outline answer to a chosen question.

Practice questions

An important aspect of exam preparation is attempting to answer past questions. If you begin early enough in your course, you can start with individual questions and build up to attempting whole papers in one session. On the other hand, you do not want to start looking at past exam papers too early and risk being discouraged because you cannot answer very many questions. If you feel that you may fall into the latter category, ask your tutor to provide examples of past questions which you should be able to tackle at that stage of the course.

It is certainly worthwhile to practice writing for the length of time which an exam involves. Many students are surprised at how quickly three hours can fly by and how difficult it is to fit in four questions in that time. Often, inexperienced students have not appreciated this and come out of their first exam saying that it was a good dress rehearsal for the resit!

Obviously the exercise of completing past questions will be more useful if you can get feedback on your performance. Ideally, one of your tutors may be persuaded to mark your answers and tell you where you went wrong. Alternatively, a self-help group can be a great source of assistance. You can swap practice answers with a group of fellow students and mark each other's work. Meetings can then be held to discuss the questions and this will help clarify the subject in your own mind and provide a different perspective. If you prefer to work alone, you could put your practice answer away for a few days, then work out a marking scheme from your notes which you can use to mark your own work. You can then see what you should have included to gain higher marks.

If time is short, you can produce essay plans, or lists of the key points you would want to include, rather than writing out the whole answer in full. This can be equally useful as questions may not come up in the same way as those you are using for revision, and it is the key points which you will want to remember in the exam. Whichever way you choose, time spent practising doing timed exam questions will certainly be time well spent.

Mock exams

Another method of preparation or practice is to have a mock examination where you answer questions under exam conditions. Often tutors will arrange these for a group of students, often half-way through the course, or sometimes as part of a formal revision period within the course. They can be very useful in pinpointing areas where further study or improved exam techniques would be beneficial. However, they are not always set at the level required by the final exam, especially if set half-way through the course. Therefore, if you pass the mocks and do not continue to progress at the same rate up to the final exams, you have no basis for assuming that you can pass the actual exams.

Examination Administration

When you think about how you will prepare for the exams, you also need to plan your personal arrangements to ensure that things go smoothly on the day.

If you are sitting the IPM national exams there are set dates by which you should have enrolled and paid the appropriate fee. These are always advertised in *PM Plus* and your tutor should also draw deadlines to your attention. Whichever exams you are taking, national or those set by your college/university, you are likely to have to arrange for time off work and to travel to the exam centre. It is in your own best interests to find out dates and times of exams as far in advance as possible, and avoid making holiday plans or major domestic changes around the time of the exams.

Make certain you know where the exam is to be held and work out how long the journey will take at that time of day. This means allowing for the worst that can happen, like fog, flat tyres and finding a parking space. If you arrive shortly after the exam has commenced, you may be admitted to the room and allowed to sit the exam but you will not be given additional time at the end to make up for time lost.

The examination centre will provide the exam answer book in which you write, but students are usually required to bring pens, pencils, and their own calculator. Different coloured pens are useful for headings and emphasis, especially if you will be doing any illustrations. Avoid felt tips which may 'bleed'. An eraser and Tipp-Ex will be useful, but do not use Tipp-Ex too liberally – putting a straight line through any unwanted points is quicker, and preferable. If you are likely to use a calculator, check that it works before entering the hall and take spare batteries with you. You may also wish to take some sweets, such as Polo mints, and tissues with you, and this is generally acceptable provided you do not irritate or disturb other students. If in doubt, you can always check with invigilators what they will allow you to bring into the exam room.

Always take with you any letters or forms you have received about the exam. These usually state your allocated examination number, which exam papers you are to take, and possibly the room in which the exam will be held. Having this information with you will help to avoid any last-minute confusion.

Exam Nerves

As the exam approaches, many students worry and may feel nervous or edgy. Apprehension is quite normal and a certain amount of anxiety can get the adrenalin flowing and sharpen the wits. However, too much stress can lead to poor performance in an exam. A well-organised study programme and well-planned revision are the two most important factors for aiding confidence. There are also relaxation techniques which can be practised in order to help cope with 'exam nerves'.

The number of candidates who suffer from serious exam nerves are in a minority. If you are in this category, you should seek advice from your tutor well before the exam. In some centres it may be possible for special arrangements to be made, for example, for you to take the exam in 'sheltered conditions' rather than in a large hall.

On the other hand, over-confidence is also to be avoided. Research has shown that students who worry a little about their performance, even though they have studied hard, probably do better than those who are complacent or who worry too much.

You should avoid causing yourself extra anxiety on the day of the exam by having a good night's sleep rather than indulging in last-minute cramming, and arrive in good time at the examination hall. If you get there early, you can always have a coffee, or go for a walk and have a last glance at your notes. It is probably a good idea at this stage to keep away from your fellow students. Discussion with others about how terrible it will be and how you are sure to fail will only add to your own anxiety. There will be plenty of time after the exam to share opinions.

EXAMPLE:
Subject revision table

Subject: *Employee Resourcing*

                         Week 1

Monday   *No revision – attending college*
Tuesday   Payment Systems
Wednesday   Pensions
Thursday   Performance-related pay
Friday
Saturday
Sunday

                         Week 2

Monday   *College*
Tuesday
Wednesday
Thursday
Friday   Human Resource Management
Saturday   Computers in Personnel
Sunday

                         Week 3

Monday   *College*
Tuesday
Wednesday   Flexible work forces
Thursday   Organisation design
Friday   Job design
Saturday
Sunday

Week 4

Monday	*College*
Tuesday	Recruitment and Selection
Wednesday	Equal Opportunities
Thursday	Appraisal systems
Friday	
Saturday	
Sunday	

References

1.   PITFIELD, M. and DONNELLY, R. *How to Take Exams.* 1980

Chapter 9

Examination techniques

In the Examination Room

For those of you who are experienced at examinations, some of this section may seem obvious. However, the points mentioned have tripped up more than one student in the past, and so are worth repeating.

You will usually find the examination paper and answer books have already been placed face down on the desks. As there will often be more than one group of students taking an exam at one time, it is important to listen carefully to any instructions about where to sit. You don't want to find yourself faced with a paper about micro-biology. Once seated, you will be instructed not to turn over the exam paper until told to do so. If anything seems missing or you have any queries, ask at this stage for assistance.

Once you are told to turn over the exam paper, and the exam has officially started, you should ensure that you have the correct exam paper: check that the title of the paper corresponds with the exam you were expecting. Any minor differences may be significant. If the invigilator needs to investigate your query by telephoning your subject tutor, the duration of the exam will be extended to make up for any time lost.

The importance of raising even what seems like a minor difference in the rubric of the exam paper can be illustrated by the following recent case. A student was taking his resit of the IPM Employee Resourcing exam at a centre where other students were taking a similar but internally assessed exam in personnel management on the same day. The candidate was unfortunately given and completed the wrong exam paper and it was only later that the mistake was identified. We don't know if the student thought the paper was incredibly difficult or amazingly easy but clearly this is the sort of incident you should take care to avoid.

It may seem obvious, but don't be tempted to cheat. The

111

invigilators will be on the look-out for any suspicious movements or furtive fumbling in a handbag or pencil case. If you are caught in what appears to be an act of cheating, you are likely to face an unpleasant exposure in front of your peers, and an investigation by the college authorities. If the evidence indicates cheating, you are likely to be barred from taking any further exams, and lose your IPM membership.

How to Tackle an Examination Paper

1. Read the paper carefully

If you have obtained copies of the past exam papers to look at before the exam, you should be familiar with the way the paper is laid out. This will help to eliminate the panic that occurs when you are confronted with an unfamiliar set of instructions. Every now and then, of course, the instructions or format of the paper will be changed, like the introduction of the compulsory integrated question in the Stage 2 national exams. But this does not happen very often, and your tutor should have given you advance warning of any changes. Where your exam paper is divided into sections, be sure that you comply with the instructions to answer *one* question from *each* section. You will automatically FAIL the paper if you don't meet this requirement.

So, you should read through the exam paper and instructions carefully and spend about five minutes thinking about which questions you might wish to answer. It is quite normal at this stage to be alarmed because you think that a favourite topic is missing, but double-check – it may just be disguised. A common mistake is to read a few words of a question, imagine that you know what is required, and then write a superb answer which will gain no marks because it has not answered the question! You cannot hope after one reading of the paper to understand the detailed implications behind each of the questions. But you should be able to identify the questions relating to those broad topic areas which you have revised.

If you do get a moment of blind panic as you open the paper, take several deep breaths. I am told that it is virtually impossible to worry and breathe deeply at the same time!

2. Select questions to answer

You need to think about how you might answer each question before making your choice. Read through all the questions slowly and carefully and give a star rating to questions which you believe you can answer. It is often useful to highlight the separate parts of a question and underline key words, so that you can see whether you can attempt all the different components of an answer. It is easy to be misled about a question and see what you want to see, rather than see what is actually there.

Sadly, within 30 seconds of receiving their papers, many students will have put circles around particular questions, and after that they rarely change their minds about which questions they are going to answer. This almost always means that they have chosen a question because they have seen a 'buzz word' in it relating to a topic they have revised. For example, a student who has revised delegation, may see the word in question 8 on the exam paper (overleaf) and write all they know about the benefits of delegation. This is unlikely to lead to a pass mark in this question, because the crucial aspect is the implications of your manager delegating to you.

All too often, students ignore questions they could answer perfectly well because they do not immediately see a familiar phrase. So, it is vital to be clear about the subject to which the question is referring and to carefully consider how you will approach answering it.

3. Decide on sequence

The next thing to do is to decide on the sequence in which you will answer the questions. If there is a compulsory question, you would be wise to answer that first, but you should read the other questions before you start writing, because they may give you ideas about how to answer the compulsory part. On the basis of your 'star rating' of questions you can number the questions in the order that you intend to answer them. In the example of the examination paper (overleaf), the student has indicated her preferences and the order in which she intends to answer them, namely questions 3, 7, 5 and 10. By doing this, the student knows that her

Institute of Personnel Management
Professional Management Foundation Programme
May 1992

MANAGEMENT PROCESSES AND FUNCTIONS

Time allowed 3 hours (+ 10 minutes reading time)

Answer four questions out of 10   All questions carry equal weighting

(Note: If a question includes reference to 'your organisation', this may be interpreted as covering any organisation with which you are familiar).

x 1. Outline what are traditionally seen as the strategic objectives of organisations in the public sector, and analyse the impact of more commercial criteria on the functioning of these organisations.

x 2. "Managers have to earn the right to manage". Discuss.

xxx 3. You have been asked to devise a one-day course in 'career planning' for a group of graduate trainees. Provide an outline of the course, and indicate clearly how it will enable you to meet the defined learning objectives.

0 4. Outline the key objectives for a marketing manager in a service organisation (e.g. retail, banking, hotels). How would s/he ensure that these objectives are met?

xx5. Indicate the principal causes of personal stress in your organisation, and suggest ways by which these may be overcome.

0 6. Describe **TWO** instances where change is occurring in your organisation. Compare and contrast the ways in which these changes are being handled, and develop guidelines for managing change in the future.

xxx 7. Identify **THREE** activities currently undertaken by your organisation which could be subcontracted to other organisations. What would be the major benefits and drawbacks of this in each case?

x 8. Write a report for your Manager suggesting how and why s/he could delegate some work to you. What might be the implications of this?

0 9. Identify the potential conflicts which may arise between different functions (e.g. production, finance, sales) in an organisation, and suggest ways in which these conflicts may be alleviated.

xx10. Imagine that your Chief Executive has suddenly developed an interest in 'green issues'. Draft an environmental policy paper for your organisation, and make recommendations for action. Justify the broad costs involved.

best work will be done first, which is important in case she runs out of time.

Many students decide to do their best question first. While this has the advantage of ease of recall of the topic, and will give you confidence, the disadvantage is that you are keyed up, tend to write too much and may even stray from the point of the question. So, if you decide to do your best question first, keep a careful watch on the time. Otherwise, you could do the best one second, by which time you will be more relaxed, and able to marshal your thoughts effectively. What is important is to tackle the questions in the sequence that you feel most comfortable with.

4. Managing the time

Once you have decided the sequence, you must work out your time allocation for each question and then monitor the time spent.

Poor time management is by far the commonest cause of failure in exams. You know before you enter the examination hall that you only have a limited amount of time in which to answer the questions, and you can work out how much time to spend on each question. You will need to allow time for reading the paper and thinking about which questions to answer, then planning time for each individual question. So, the amount of time you will actually have available for writing is quite limited. You do not need to write long answers of several pages in order to get good marks: some of the highest marks go to short answers provided they are relevant and well structured. Of course, much depends on your handwriting, but as a rough guide, Derek Torrington says: 'An answer that hangs together in 1.5 pages is going to say more than one that rambles over 4 or more.' Most students will write answers two to three sides long.

The IPM national exams are all three hours long plus 10 minutes' reading time. There is notionally a period of ¾ hour for each question, but allowing for initial planning and then reflecting on what you have written, you will be writing at most for 35 minutes per question. You should jot down a timetable for the three-hour period and stick to it, because it is essential that you answer all four questions. Some students think that if they answer three questions very well, they will get a good mark. Regrettably they are just as likely to fail the exam overall. This can be shown by an explanation of the exam marking system.

Typically you will be sitting an exam with four questions, each carrying 25 out of a possible 100 marks available for the whole exam. To pass the exam you will need to get 50 marks or more and an average of 13 marks per question. The examiners will have a marking scheme which indicates how many marks are awarded for a marginal, pass, good pass and distinction level answer. It will be fairly easy to get the first few marks, say 6–8 points. Even on a question about which you are not too happy, coverage of some of the basic points will gain you some marks. If you do not attempt it, you will get no marks. Conversely, if you spend time perfecting another question, you might raise what is already a pass (say 13/25) by a few marks (to 16/25), but this would be unlikely to achieve the same number of marks as starting on a new question (6–8 points). If your overall performance is marginal, the good question will not be sufficient to bring you up to a pass.

It is therefore essential that you spend a reasonable amount of time on each question, and never inadvertently leave yourself no time to answer one or more questions. Keep a close watch on the clock to ensure that each question is attempted.

5. Read each selected question carefully

Half the battle in any exam is understanding what an examiner wants. Study of past exam papers will familiarise you with the types of questions, and discussion with your tutor and fellow students should have helped you understand the different ways of approaching a question. In the chapter on assignments we looked at what is involved in writing and the points made are relevant for exams too.

We pointed out that it is not sufficient to write down everything you know. That is called the 'mud at the wall' answer, because the student presents all they know on the topic in the hope that some of it will hit the target. What is required is that you make your answer relevant to the question asked, and can apply your knowledge to an organisational situation or problem. We shall use the following question as an example of the approach you should take.

EXAMPLE QUESTION

Discuss the characteristics a group should possess in order to maximise its work potential.

This is a seemingly simple question, but there is a lot contained within it. Key words/phrases are 'characteristics of a group' and 'work potential', and the instruction is to discuss how one can be maximised by the other. Questions which should come to mind in considering this question are:

- What are the characteristics of a group?
- Which characteristics will help maximise work potential?
- Will these characteristics always have this result?
- If not, why not? Is the context relevant?
- What else will be needed in order to maximise work potential?
- What examples from my own experience will illustrate my understanding?

The 'discuss' and 'should' terminology implies that the relationship between the two aspects of the question may not be straightforward. In the answer the two aspects should be clarified, and a balanced argument should be put forward drawing on your knowledge and personal experience.

Any student who merely wrote down a list of characteristics of effective work groups would gain few marks. Although they would have shown they knew the 'ideal' situation, they would not have demonstrated that they understood the effect of context and the implications of the question. So, the example illustrates that it is vital you spend time understanding what the question is asking for, and identifying all the different parts which should be addressed, rather than just remembering and reproducing all the details of the topic.

6. Prepare a plan

Time spent thinking through and planning your answer is never wasted, provided you have worked out how much time you should allocate to each question. As we said above, you will gain more marks for a coherent and well-structured piece of work than one which seems like a series of unconnected points.

You will probably have lots of ideas racing around your head. Jot them down in rough before you lose them. Here again, a mind map may be useful to you, or you may prefer to list key words. Occasionally students may write a very detailed plan and leave too little time to actually write it up, so there has to be a balance.

EXAMPLE QUESTION

Discuss the characteristics a group should possess in order to maximise its work potential

Jottings

group cohesion – promote	size
	detract	homogeneity
		task e.g. danger e.g. miners

outside influences – threat/competition

proximity
remuneration
leadership

Outline Plan

Typical Components of Plan	*Plan for this Question*

1. Introduction
   What is the question about?
   How am I going to tackle it?
	1. Intro
	   I will first describe the
	   factors which promote/
	   detract from effectiveness
	   . . . then . . . leading to
	   general conclusions on . . .

2. Define key terms/concepts in
   the question
	2. Group characteristics e.g.
	   size, homogeneity . . .
	   Work potential – output –
	   job satisfaction.

---

3. Main part of answer referring to appropriate published sources and examples	3. Importance of group cohesion – depends on task, proximity, danger e.g. miners, remuneration, leadership. External influences e.g. competition. How management can harness group effort towards work goals.
4. Conclusion: relating clearly to the question	4. To maximise work potential, both internal features of groups and external factors have to be considered and managed.

The plan should be written in the answer book, on a clean page, on the left-hand side opposite the page where you will start to write. This has the advantage of ease of reference during those first few crucial sentences as you get into the swing of the answer.

Of course, you do not need to follow your plan slavishly. As you write, you will often find that further ideas come to mind and, provided you have enough time, you can incorporate them into your answer.

Once you have written your answer, you should put a clear line through the plan. Examiners are not supposed to pay attention to work that has been crossed through, but if they are seeking to give you the benefit of the doubt, or the extra mark you need to pass, they may refer to your notes to see what you were trying to cover. This point should also be remembered if you are running out of time with an answer: make sure your notes are legible and indicate that you have run out of time.

Incidentally, some students spend valuable time writing out the question in their answer book. While cosmetically this looks nicer, it is not necessary and won't gain any extra marks. So don't bother unless you find it especially helpful to you. Some students do say that it helps to calm them down and concentrate their minds. However, all that is required is to indicate clearly the number of the question you are attempting in the margin at the beginning of the answer.

7. Structure your answer

Examiners can often identify the student who did not plan their answer, but began writing almost immediately, because they will write for several pages and about two paragraphs before the end they will say 'and therefore the answer to the question is . . .'

The plan illustrated (page 118) shows that you need to start off with an introduction, to show you comprehend the question. Although there is no standard format to be followed, the sorts of things to include are:

• an outline of your understanding of the question if it is liable to different interpretations; or
• a comment on the views represented by the question; or
• a brief statement of what you intend to write about.

You should think about your conclusion, as well as your introduction, before you start writing, in order to avoid a regurgitation of the introduction, or even worse, tailing off without any conclusion. Remember that the introduction is the first thing the examiner reads and sets the scene, creating a good (or bad) initial impression, in much the same way as a first impression in selection interviews. The conclusion is the last thing the examiner reads before a mark is allocated, so a well-structured answer leading to a clear conclusion is likely to gain a better mark.

As in writing assignments, you will find that subheadings make the structure of your argument clearer. Heading each new paragraph with a key word or phrase can be very useful to you and your examiner in following a line of thought. Diagrams can also be usefully included as part of your answer. Try, for example, to explain Kolb or Honey and Mumford's learning cycle without being able to draw it! However, don't worry about aiming for artistic perfection in your drawing – it is simply important to show you understand the ideas.

Many IPM exam questions will ask for the answer to be presented in a particular format, e.g. a report or a memo to management. In which case, marks will be awarded for following this instruction. If a report or memo is required, make sure you indicate who it is to/from, title it, and for a report give a list of contents. If a question asks you to prepare a presentation, you will be expected to indicate how you will introduce your talk to your audience and keep their attention, what visual aids or other resources you may make use of, as well as actually writing out the contents of the presentation. If a question involves calculations, show your working out as well as the result, as you will pick up marks for doing it in the right way, even if you get the wrong answer.

8. Keep on track

While you are writing, keep checking that you are not straying away from the question you are trying to answer. Re-read the question at regular intervals to make sure you are keeping to the main point. You can demonstrate to the examiners that you are staying on track by using key words from the question. For example, in the question illustrated above, we could use phrases or sentences such as:

> . . . one of the significant <u>characteristics</u> is <u>group</u> cohesion
> . . . outside influences such as external threats or competition may affect <u>group</u> cohesion.
> . . . competition can have positive or negative consequences for <u>group</u> functioning.
> . . . a <u>group</u> may not necessarily direct its efforts to the achievement of <u>work</u>/organisational goals.
> . . . <u>work potential</u> will be affected by the nature of the task and physical proximity.
> . . . to <u>maximise</u> <u>work potential</u>, there should be a common goal.

At the same time you should try and write in an easy and free flowing style. Avoid continually repeating certain words or starting sentences with the same words such as 'therefore' or 'consequently' or 'in conclusion'.

As with answering assignments, you are trying to show that you know and understand the concepts taught on the course, and can apply them to a situation or problem. Whenever you make a statement, back it with reasoned argument and avoid oversimplified generalisations. It is not necessary to memorise lists of authors and quotations, but you should indicate the name of key commentators wherever possible. While your own opinions are relevant, you should not substitute them for informed and logical evidence, or what is regarded as 'best practice', without any reasoned back-up for your position.

Equally, it is inappropriate in questions which ask you to 'refer to an organisation with which you are familiar' to describe in an uncritical fashion the way it is done. For example, if you are asked to design an appraisal scheme for your employing organisation, do not answer that your organisation already has one and describe it. Instead you should indicate what you would recommend, and draw on successful and less successful aspects from your employers' scheme as illustrations of the points you are trying to make.

Sometimes you may feel that you are running out of steam on a question. You may be tempted to waffle on and try and pad out the answer. It is much more sensible to go on to another question and come back later. Coming again to the question from a different standpoint may in fact result in new insights which you had not been aware of earlier.

9. Write legibly

It seems such an obvious point, but if the examiners can't read your writing, you won't get the marks you anticipated. You should remember that the examiner will have a large batch of scripts to mark in a very short time. For the IPM exams, an examiner may have several hundred scripts to be read and marked in the space of two to three weeks. While it is accepted that working neatly under the pressure of exam conditions is not easy, no examiner likes to struggle to read one word after another. In the vast majority of cases, the writing can be deciphered, but if not, many of the points made will be missed. So, legibility is vital, and there are several things you can do to help yourself.

- Practise writing legibly at speed well before your exams. Get a colleague to read some of your writing and say whether it is easy to read.
- Use a pen which you know will force you to write more neatly. Some students use a fountain pen instead of a ball point, but you have to balance this against slowing down the amount of information you can get down on paper.

- Write in larger script, and/or use only alternate lines on the page.
- Leave some time to go back over your answers at the end of the exam and clarify any key words or phrases which are illegible.
- If your writing problem has a medical cause, consult your tutor in advance, as it may be possible for you to type or dictate an answer. These sort of arrangements take some time and the appropriate authority may be needed from within your college or the IPM.

You are not penalised for handing in answer books with large areas crossed out. This is often unavoidable, and as long as that section of the answer is clearly scored out, the examiners will ignore it.

10. If you run out of time

It has already been stressed that it is much more important to attempt all four questions than to perfect any particular answer. If, despite your best intentions, you find yourself running out of time on a question, you should leave it and go on to the next. However, it is a good idea to leave some blank pages in the answer book before starting the next question, so that you can come back and finish later. You will usually find that, over the exam as a whole, you can readjust your timetable and have enough time to adequately address the four questions.

If you realise you are seriously short of time and will not be able to complete the last question, you should adopt the following strategy. If say, you have only 15 minutes left, you should spend the time available jotting down a plan of the answer you would have written. It is a good idea to write on the page 'ran out of time – answer plan only'. Most examiners will give you credit for the key points you are able to cover, and if you leave plenty of space between the points you can go back over and add more in and write out your introduction and conclusion. It is not worth writing personal notes to the examiner giving excuses as to why you did not do better as these will be ignored.

Most students find that the time goes amazingly quickly and they could have written for longer. A handful of students finish well before the end of the exam. Many centres will have a rule that no one may leave the room in the last half hour of the exam, so as to avoid disturbing other students. If this is the case, it will be announced at the appropriate time. However, even if not, you should resist the temptation to leave the examination hall. Instead, you should use the time to go over and over your answers, adding to them and improving them, checking your handwriting and spelling.

Chapter 10

What to do if things go wrong

We have said in previous chapters that if despite all your plans and good intentions, things don't quite work out, you should talk over your difficulties and don't let problems build up. So if you are having difficulties with course material, talk to the subject tutor. If you are having workload problems in general, talk to the Course Director. If you encounter problems that interfere with your exam preparation, let your college know at once. If you have an accident on your way to the exam, let your Course Director know as soon as possible. Make contact with your tutors throughout the course: they want you to pass.

However, there are other things that can go wrong which we haven't covered, such as dissatisfaction with your course, and failing the exams.

Complaints About Your Course

If you are dissatisfied with any aspect of your course, you should take steps to make that dissatisfaction known, so that the institution can do something to improve the situation.

Part of the IPM course approval process is to require colleges to have monitoring and review arrangements, including:

- A professional adviser, nominated in consultation with the local IPM branch, who attends meetings with staff and students;
- Student representatives elected by students;
- Staff–student consultative committee;
- End of year course report prepared by teaching team;
- Course report considered by course committee/board of studies.

Colleges are also required to have a grievance procedure which involves the professional adviser, and an appeals procedure for assessments, which involves the external examiners.

If you have a problem or grievance you should take it up through the appropriate channels – as you would advise any employee who seeks advice from you in the personnel department. If however you feel you are getting nowhere and have exhausted the available procedures, you can always contact the Education Department at IPM head office, which monitors the quality of programmes. This of course only happens in a few cases because problems are normally resolved amicably by informal contacts between staff and students.

Failing the Exams

Failing an exam most usually comes about because a student did not do enough study and revision. Occasionally a student who is regarded as very able by tutors and other students fails an exam, even in their area of expertise. For example, I know an employee relations adviser who failed the Employee Relations paper and a training manager who failed the Employee Development paper, yet both passed the other two exams! The cause of the failure could be attributed to one or more reasons.

One view is that the failure is due to a fault in the assessment criteria. Both individuals were regarded as highly competent by their respective employers, but the examination was drawing on different skills from those which they used at work. They could be very good in face-to-face situations in the workplace, but could not apply their extensive experience to a hypothetical situation which demanded a concise, written answer in under 45 minutes.

Another cause can be complacency. Students will revise more thoroughly in the areas they are less familiar with and tend to skimp on those they are more confident of. For this reason, many students, to their surprise, pass Management Information Systems!

The reaction of a confident student may be to appeal, which may be possible if you have sat exams which are assessed locally at your college. Most professional bodies do not enter into correspondence on individual exam results. The IPM takes the following approach for the national exams:

- Examination results are moderated to ensure consistency of approach between markers and between examination sessions.
- Examiners' reports on the standards and results of each examination are published. These will be automatically sent to you with the results of the examination you fail. The reports will provide general indicators of where students have gone wrong and can be especially beneficial to discuss with your college tutor before attempting the exam again.
- On the payment of a fee to the IPM Education Department, students can apply to be sent the Chief Examiner's comments on their paper(s). This could be particularly helpful if you feel you have revised adequately, yet you have failed, and you want to identify where you are going wrong. A list of the typical comments is given in Appendix F (page 128).
- A Course Director, on payment of a fee to the IPM, can be sent an analysis of the exam performance of the group of students from that institution. This would be useful to track down particular areas of the syllabus where the tutor's approach is different from that taken by the Chief Examiner, or where students are having difficulties in grasping particular concepts.

If you find you have failed an exam, seek advice and try again. Contact your Course Director and find out whether tuition is available for students in your circumstances. If not, see if individual tutors would be willing to go through the relevant examination paper with you. Also contact fellow students who are also going to do resits, and see if you can form a revision self-help group along the lines described in Chapter 2.

Appendix F

Reasons why answers may fail

Content

- Insufficient answer to question
- Poor-quality answers
- Insufficient knowledge of subject matter
- Inaccurate answer
- Inadequate coverage of field
- Insufficient recognition of commercial realities
- Level of answer too general
- Lack of understanding of issues
- Failure to provide examples to illustrate a point
- Lack of reference to sources

Skills

- Failure to answer question(s) set
- Lack of practical approach
- Lack of management approach
- Poor legibility
- Poor presentation/grammar
- Lack of persuasiveness/argument
- Inadequate maturity of approach
- Lack of creativity
- Where there is a multi-part question, failure to adequately answer each part
- Poor timing

Chapter 11

The Professional Management Foundation Programme

The Professional Management Foundation Programme (PMFP) is based on the premise that all managers, including personnel staff, are managers first and functional specialists second. Therefore those beginning to study management need to develop a broad-based understanding of the principles, processes and skills of management in general before going on to study their particular management specialism.

The design of the PMFP was influenced by developments or thinking about management education and management development, especially the Handy report and the Management Charter Initiative. These identified that managerial work takes place at three main levels within organisations: operational, professional and strategic. The PMFP is targeted at the operational level and aims to cover general managerial issues which are relevant to all managers.

The standard to be aimed at in answering examination questions is that of a university pass degree or equivalent. This means that you must demonstrate a clear understanding of the basic concepts, literature and material that underpin your studies and be capable of presenting analyses and arguments in a systematic and logical fashion. All questions on exam papers carry an equal weighting, although within a question there may be two or more sub-parts which may have a different weighting depending on the nature of the question.

All exam papers ask you to make reference to 'your organisation', which may be interpreted as covering any organisation with which you are familiar. So, if you are not presently in employment, you can refer to a voluntary organisation of which you are a member, a previous employer, or the educational establishment where you are studying, if you find that these provide appropriate practical examples. Alternatively, you may draw on case studies which are discussed in class or which you come across in your reading. The important thing to remember is that the PMFP is a managerial qualification and therefore you should relate your answers to practical situations and you should take a managerial approach. This means diagnosing problems and opportunities, 'owning' ideas and not implying that 'they' should change, and providing realistic and creative solutions and recommendations to the situations or problems you are presented with.

The PMFP is made up of four modules and this chapter will take each in turn, provide some general guidance about the approach to the exam paper, indicate important areas of the syllabus which you should cover in your revision, and give examples of the types of questions you will be asked.

Management Processes and Functions

The Management Processes and Functions module is central to the whole concept of the Professional Management Foundation Programme and covers subject areas which underpin the study of the other three modules. In many colleges, Management Processes and Functions is taught together with the Managing Human Resources module, because there is a common group of theories and concepts which apply to both. At the same time, an understanding of management functions will put into context the need for management information systems, and help you relate to the wider, corporate environment in which management functions are carried out.

Management Processes and Functions aims to give a basic introduction to management, and how this is practised in organisations. On completion of the module you should understand why management has evolved as an occupation and what managerial work involves. You should also have gained some general managerial skills such as being able to work effectively as a member of a group and present a coherent proposal in a written or oral form.

Syllabus topics

Management Processes and Functions divides into four sections and there will be one if not two questions on each of these sections.

Management of self

This covers the nature of management and how to manage performance, as well as aspects of personal effectiveness in your job and career. Hopefully, many of the topics are already well known to you, so you can start your studies by making sense of your own reality and position in the organisation. Typical topics and questions are likely to be:

- Nature of managerial work

  'Managerial work is typically characterised by brevity, variety and fragmentation.' How well does this apply to your own job (or one with which you are familiar) and how do you minimise the problems which this can create?

  Write a report for your manager suggesting how and why s/he could delegate some work to you. What might be the implications of this?

- Managing performance, setting targets and objectives

  Outline the key objectives for a line manager in a firm manufacturing high quality products. How would s/he ensure that these objectives are met?

  Outline the key objectives for a purchasing manager in an organisation which produces low cost/high volume products. How would s/he ensure that these objectives are met?

- A well-known technique for analysis is SWOT

  Conduct a SWOT (Strengths, Weaknesses, Opportunities, Threats) analysis for your organisation, and indicate why this might be a useful project to undertake.

- Personnel effectiveness, including time management, stress management, and career planning

You have been asked to devise a one-day course on 'time management' for a group of senior managers. Provide an outline of the course, and indicate clearly how it will enable you to meet the defined learning objectives.

Indicate the principal causes of personal stress in your organisation, and suggest ways by which these may be overcome.

Working with other people

This involves an understanding of the demands placed on any manager when working with other people, and some essential skills for being effective. Typical topics and questions are likely to be:

- Writing a report and running or taking part in committee meetings

   Write a report for your boss indicating how departmental (or other similar types of) meetings in your organisation can be made more effective.

   Analyse the major reasons why committee meetings often fail to achieve results. What can be done to minimise the likelihood of failure?

   Identify the major problems which the Chair is likely to encounter in organising and running committee meetings, and explain how these problems might be overcome.

- The need to manage change, gain the commitment of others and communicate effectively

   'Managers have to earn the right to manage.' Discuss.

   Describe TWO instances where change is occurring in your organisation. Compare and contrast the ways in which these changes are being handled, and develop guidelines for managing change in the future.

   Imagine that your organisation is just about to introduce a briefing system, and that you have been allocated responsibility for preparing the core brief to staff. What information would be contained in this first brief, and why would it be included?

The remaining two areas may be less well known to you, but are essential to your understanding of how your employing organisation operates.

Management functions

This gives an understanding of the principal functions in your organisation, the different ways of organising these functions into a structure, and the conflicts which may break out. Typical topics and questions are likely to be:

* Managerial functions and activities

  Analyse the key activities undertaken by the finance OR research and development functions in your organisation. Compare and contrast these with another organisation with which you are familiar, and account for any differences or similarities.

  Identify THREE activities currently undertaken by your organisation which could be subcontracted to other organisations. What would be the major benefits and drawbacks of this in each case?

* Implications of changes in organisation structure such as decentralisation or matrix structures

  Explain what is meant by a matrix organisation structure, and analyse its effectiveness compared with more traditional organisation structures.

  Analyse the managerial considerations which need to be taken into account when deciding whether to decentralise decision-making in a multidivisional organisation to unit level.

  Define BRIEFLY what is meant by the term 'Total Quality Management'. Evaluate the impact of TQM on the structure and culture of your organisation.

* Organisational politics, conflict between functions and how to overcome them

What is meant by the term 'organisational politics'? Assess whether or not organisational politics can ever have a positive impact on performance.

Identify the major arguments for and against managers moving between functions (for example, personnel, production, marketing) on one or more occasions during their careers.

Identify the potential conflicts which may arise between different functions (e.g. production, finance, sales) in an organisation, and suggest ways in which these conflicts may be alleviated.

Strategy in the organisation

This gives an insight into the major components of corporate strategy and how it affects the day-to-day practice of management, for example in mission statements. Typical topics and questions are likely to be:

- Strategic objectives in organisations

  What are the principal strategic objectives of your organisation? How appropriate are these objectives given the environment in which the organisation operates?

  Outline what are traditionally seen as the strategic objectives of organisations in the public sector, and analyse the impact of more commercial criteria on the functioning of these organisations.

  Prepare a mission statement for your organisation, explain why this might be of value, and indicate how it might be disseminated throughout the whole organisation.

- Contemporary issues like social responsibility, customer care, privatisation and 'green' issues

  What do you understand by the term 'social responsibility'? How might socially responsible practices vary between a manufacturing firm and a retail outlet?

  Define BRIEFLY the term 'customer care'. Analyse the impact

of customer care on the structure and culture of your organisation.

Analyse the way in which privatisation is likely to change the strategic objectives of an organisation.

Imagine that your Chief Executive has suddenly developed an interest in 'green issues'. Draft an environmental policy paper for your organisation, and make recommendations for action. Justify the broad costs involved.

Types of questions

Overall, the paper is a mix of theory and practice in that some questions will test your awareness of concepts and others will emphasise practical applications. There is always a balance between questions which ask you to relate an issue or concept to your employing organisation, and questions dealing with more hypothetical situations. Examples of the former include:

> Indicate the principal causes of personal stress in your organisation, and suggest ways by which these may be overcome.

And of the latter:

> Outline the key objectives for a marketing manager in a service organisation (e.g. retail, banking, hotels). How would s/he ensure that these objectives are met?

There will also be questions which can be answered by a more general approach, for example:

> Evaluate how the following functions 'add value' to your organisation:
> a) finance
> b) personnel
> c) marketing

and questions which require you to show an awareness of contemporary issues in the area of management. You will need to read newspapers and journal articles regularly to supplement the key texts on the booklist both to keep abreast of current topics which may be the focus of a question, and to pick up 'buzz words' which you could include in your answers.

As well as a question from each section, the examiner usually includes a broader question which tests wider understanding of concepts relevant to the whole PMFP, for example:

> Analyse the key activities undertaken by the finance OR research and development functions in your organisation. Compare and contrast these with another organisation with which you are familiar, and account for any differences or similarities.

This type of question requires you to consider the activities of a function/individual other than the personnel department/manager, and analyse these in relation to their place in the organisation. The examiner's report indicates that such questions will be a regular feature of the Management Processes and Functions examinations because the ability to compare and contrast activities, and account for any differences, is an essential analytical approach required in management.

> This question goes to the very heart of the PMFP philosophy, in that it requires students to consider the activities of a function/ individual other than the personnel department/manager, and analyse these in relation to its place within the organisation. It seems to me that anyone ought to be able to describe their own activities or, with the benefit of a good memory, reproduce two pages of a textbook. However, trying to compare and contrast activities, and account for any differences, is what the study of management is all about. On the basis of the answers produced here, very few of the candidates possess this wider perspective. Students should be aware that I will continue to ask questions such as this despite (or perhaps because of) their lack of popularity because they are so essential for encouraging this more analytical approach to management.

Questions are often made up of several parts, and each part has to be answered to gain a high mark. For example, in the question illustrated above which asks you to evaluate how the finance, personnel and marketing functions 'add value' to your organisation, each part will carry equal marks. In the following question, the first part which asks you to define a concept is important, but it will have less weight than the remainder which asks you to relate this to practical situations.

> Explain what is meant by a 'brainstorming exercise', and identify the situations in which this is most likely to be effective. What are the major advantages and disadvantages of brainstorming?

The best students according to the examiner's report answered all parts of the question, first by defining the term itself, before going on to deal with the situation in which it was most likely to be effective (training programmes, new design ideas, creative situations, etc.), and discussing its major advantages and disadvantages. This seemed a reasonable enough way to answer the question, so students who did this generally got through. Those who failed this question either did not define the term, missed out one or more parts of the question, or listed advantages and disadvantages without any attempt to relate these to the previous part of the question.

The questions are put in a variety of formats. Typically, they demand an essay-type approach. There are also questions which ask for a report, a presentation or an outline for a one-day course. Remember that if the question asks for a particular format, this should be used, otherwise your answer will fail, irrespective of the quality of what is written.

A report-type question

> Write a short report entitled 'How to write an effective report'

In order to pass, this should be written with sections such as an executive summary, main body, conclusions and recommendations and appendices. Good answers included the importance of the work prior to drafting the report, and allowing time to reflect on the contents and redraft on one or more occasions.

A presentation-type question

> You have been asked to make a short presentation to a group
> of 16-year-old students about the nature of managerial work.
> What would you say in order to convey a realistic impression
> to them?

As well as outlining relevant theories about management, the
answer to this type of question should indicate that you understand
the importance of tailoring your talk to the needs of the audience.
This would include giving appropriate examples, in the context of
a school/college environment, or the part-time jobs which students
may be undertaking. You can also outline the methods of
presentation you would use, for example, flip charts, film clips,
quiz questions, group work etc.

A course outline-type question

> You have been asked to devise a one-day course in 'career
> planning' for a group of graduate trainees. Provide an outline
> of the course, and indicate clearly how it will enable you to
> meet the defined learning objectives.

To answer this, you would set out clearly the objectives for the
one-day course, then briefly outline the programme before going
on to relate the activities in the programme to the objectives you
have defined. Merely writing out a timetable for the day with little
detail other than '10.30–11.30: group exercise' and '1.00–2.00:
lunch' would not achieve a pass mark.

Corporate Environment

The Corporate Environment module aims to give a basic understanding of the external environment in which organisations in
both the public and private sector operate, and the effect this has
on management practice. On completion of the module you
should be able to identify the principal economic, social, political
and legal influences on decision-making in organisations. You will
be able to analyse an organisation's activities alongside infor-

mation from external sources in order to prepare forecasts of the likely consequences for the business.

The Corporate Environment module, as with all PMFP modules, provides an academic building block for Stage 2, and you will find your study of economic and political factors very relevant to the Employee Relations 1 and 2 modules. Legal and social factors will be particularly helpful as a foundation for Employee Resourcing 1 and 2 modules. The examiner has commented that candidates do tend to avoid the economic and political questions, and if this means that they are less well prepared for these parts of the syllabus, they could be disadvantaged in their Stage 2 studies.

The examiner looks to see that students are able to demonstrate a basic understanding of the concepts incorporated in the syllabus, and are able to apply them in an organisational context. It is important to be up-to-date and know what is currently happening in 'the corporate environment'. You can do this by reading beyond the core textbook, and skimming the quality newspapers, business and professional journals to keep abreast of current issues. You are also advised to watch relevant television documentaries and critically evaluate their contribution to our understanding of the corporate environment. In addition, you can use examples from your course work assignments in order to illustrate the effects of the external environment on organisations.

Syllabus topics

The Corporate Environment module is in five sections. The current pattern is that there is one question on Section 1, and two questions from each of the remaining four sections. The final question is normally a general one, or perhaps a topical one, in order to give candidates an opportunity to show their overall understanding of the module as a whole.

The corporate setting

This covers corporate culture and issues of ownership and the effect on the management of the organisation. There is often a question on an aspect of ownership. Typical questions are likely to be:

'A (corporate) culture cannot be precisely defined, for it is something that is perceived, something felt' (Handy 1985). Discuss.

'Who owns an organisation is irrelevant in terms of how it is managed.' Discuss.

The first question requires a knowledge of the writings of Charles Handy, and can be complemented by comparing them with the work of Deal and Kennedy. The second question is not a 'disguised' one focusing on corporate culture, as some students thought. It offers an opportunity to demonstrate knowledge of how the different forms of private and public ownership affect corporate policy, financial management and marketing. The comparative method which was explained in Chapter 6 would be a suitable approach to answering this question. Much could have been said about foreign-owned companies, such as Japanese and American ones, and their often distinctive styles of management associated with managing quality, single union recognition, non-union firms, as well as their approaches to personnel and human resource management.

Social factors

This involves an understanding of the effects of demographic trends on the working population, and equal opportunities issues. Typical questions are likely to be:

What demographic trends are affecting organisations in the early 1990s? How are organisations responding to them?

What are the obstacles to achieving 'equality of opportunity' within organisations?

Questions on 'demographic trends' provide an opportunity to use practical examples from your own organisation, showing how recruitment, selection, training and other personnel policies are likely to be affected by population changes.

'Equal opportunity' questions can usually be examined fairly widely in terms of gender, race, marital status, disability and age although occasionally a question may be concerned with particular groups, such as ethnic minorities. The questions usually focus on how best practice might be achieved in organisations and offer an opportunity to discuss individual, collective, cultural and institutional prejudices.

Economic factors

This gives an insight into the macro-economic environment and how it has affected your organisation. A question will often be formed around the influence of government economic policies.

The second question in this section is often to do with the role of markets and the main features of the mixed economy as compared with a free-market economy. This enables an examination of the potential conflicts between equality and efficiency in the resource allocation process. Typical questions are likely to be:

How economically successful was the Government's macro-economic policy in the 1980s?

'A mixed economy is fairer than a free-market economy in allocating scarce resources but less efficient in using them.' Discuss.

Political factors

This is concerned with the political system of 'liberal democracy' within which Western organisations operate, and questions may bring in the influence of the European Community. A second question in this section often concerns interest or pressure groups, such as employer groups or trade unions, and how such organisations can influence government policy. As we said earlier, this topic is very relevant to Employee Relations at Stage 2, with the changing roles of Britain's central employer and union confederations being a key issue. Typical questions on political factors include:

What are the distinctive features of 'liberal democracy' as a political system? Outline some of the implications of liberal democracy for the corporate sector.

To what extent is it true to say that the Confederation of British Industry and the Trades Union Congress have been marginalised as industrial pressure groups in recent years?

Legal factors

This gives a basic introduction to law, especially the law of contracts and the main aspects of employment law which managers should be aware of. Employment law is studied in greater depth at Stage 2. Typical questions are likely to be:

'Contracts are at the root of all business relations.' Discuss.

What are the main statutory employment rights of employees?

The question on contracts requires not just an outline of the main characteristics of contract law, but also an examination of the practical implications of contracts for business relations including the regulation of employment relations, business transactions and relations between suppliers and customers. Recent changes in public sector purchasing arrangements could be used as examples.

The question on employment rights may appear to be a nice, easy descriptive question. According to the examiner's report, however, responses tended to be disappointing, with many candidates providing 'long litanies of employment protection rights which, in some cases, were not particularly accurate in content'. It is obviously important to be as up-to-date as possible and not to wander around the point.

The general question

This usually requires you to bring together all the factors at work in the corporate environment and consider how they are affecting your employing organisation. This type of question gives you an opportunity to draw on your understanding of the module as a whole, bring in relevant examples from your work experience and course work assignments, and show the links between theory and practice, concepts and applications. Typical questions include:

Identify the main external influences affecting your organisation. Illustrate how changes in one of these influences have affected your organisation recently.

Analyse TWO areas where your organisation has been affected by its external environment in the last year and how it has responded.

This question enables you to bring in your understanding of topical issues, for example, the Single European Market, environmental and green issues or the impact of recession, legislation, fiscal policy, compulsory competitive tendering, corporate takeovers, and so forth.

Types of questions

Questions aim to test your understanding of the ideas and concepts which underpin the syllabus, as well as giving you an opportunity to demonstrate your skills of analysis and evaluation. Questions will normally require you to do both, by relating the topic of the question to your own organisation and professional experience. Even if the question does not actually say 'with examples drawn from your organisation', you should always consider the implication of the topic for managerial and corporate decision-making. So, for example, in the following question, you would lose valuable marks if you did not give examples of the implications of liberal democracy for your own or other employing organisations.

What are the distinctive features of 'liberal democracy' as a political system? Outline some of the implications of liberal democracy for the corporate sector.

Generally, you are encouraged to bring in your own work experiences and reflect your own views and value systems in answers, but you should also be able to critically evaluate them.

Questions are often in two parts, and each part has to be answered to give high marks, although the relative weighting between the parts depends on the nature of the question set. In the question above, on liberal democracy, even if the first part were outstanding, it would be difficult to gain a high mark if you did not satisfactorily address the second part.

The format of questions in the Corporate Environment paper is usually an essay style, asking you to discuss an issue, analyse the impact on your organisation, or compare and contrast two different ways of looking at a topic. Guidance on how to address these types of questions has been given in Chapters 6 and 9.

Managing Human Resources

The Managing Human Resources module aims to give you an understanding of how the behavioural sciences can be applied to your work environment. You will gain a basic grounding in the disciplines of psychology and sociology and the relevance of these to the analysis and solution of behavioural problems in organisations. On completion of the module, you should be able to analyse your learning processes and implement strategies to enhance your self-development. You will also gain knowledge and skills in interviewing and counselling poor performers, and analysing and improving the behaviour of groups.

In setting the question paper, the examiner is seeking to test three areas of competence. Firstly, you are expected to show a grasp of the theories and concepts underpinning the module. You will find that questions sometimes involve quotations from the recommended textbooks, and therefore you are advised to be familiar with these texts.

Secondly, the examiner is looking for an ability to apply the theories, concepts, principles and techniques you have learned to some specific scenarios which are outlined in the questions. It is not sufficient just to explain the relevant theories, you will have to apply them to the practical situation which is presented in the question. So, even where the question doesn't actually ask you for examples from your own experience or employing organisation, you are expected to look for opportunities to incorporate examples and illustrative material into your answers.

Your examples can be drawn from both work or non-work organisations, from your educational experience and family, or from familiarity with organisational events which have been publicised in the media. The examiner takes the line that there is no excuse for scripts which are long on theory and short on practice. Accepting that some students may not be working in personnel, or working at all, it is suggested that there are compensating activities which can be undertaken. These include attendance at IPM branch meetings, which can help establish a network of contacts, and reading *Personnel Management* (especially the corporate case studies) and other journals and newspapers, as well as books with anecdotal material.

Where your examples are drawn from experience, you should take a critical approach. It will not be sufficient, for example, to describe the selection procedures used by your current employers. You should offer ideas for improvement even when describing current practice.

Thirdly, the examiner is looking for answers which demonstrate that candidates are aware of current issues and causes for debate amongst human resource practitioners. Reading journals and newspaper articles will help here too. The examiner emphasises that answers must be founded in reality, and the reality for most organisations is that they are operating in a climate of scarce resources and often faced with competitive pressures. Therefore answers should reflect a realistic attitude and the likelihood that behavioural issues may not always receive a high priority.

Syllabus topics

The module is divided into three main sections. In the examination, there will be at least two questions from each of these sections, and it is likely that certain questions will require knowledge drawn from more than one section. For example, questions on personality and motivation are likely to relate to two of the sections.

Individual behaviour

One of the more 'academic' type questions concerns the topic of personality and how it is defined, for example:

> Weightman argues that there are three main schools of thought on personality: psychoanalysis, behaviourism, and humanistic psychology. What are the essential constituents of each? What insights can they offer about behaviour in organisations?

Combined with an issue from another section, it becomes a more practical question, for example:

> In what ways do psychologists and lay people differ when they use the term 'personality'? To what extent is it appropriate or productive to try to assess and measure 'personality' in the selection process?

Occupational choice and orientations to work are common themes in the examination, but the questions usually ask for a practical focus in terms of the implications for human resource policies, for example:

> What is 'alienation'? To what extent can the presence or absence of alienation among organisational employees be empirically demonstrated and measured? What are the implications for the management of your organisation?

> What are the factors affecting occupational choice? What are the implications of these factors for the effective management of people?

The examiner's report makes some revealing comments on responses to this last question:

> The worst answers were those which (yet again) pontificated about Maslow's hierarchy of needs, which is still presented as if it is empirical fact rather than kite-flying hypothesis. The poor answers also incorporated naive and simplistic observations: 'If the occupation has a good salary, this can be a motive for choosing this career' . . . Only a few scripts made any detailed reference to the situation in the labour market, or even suggested there are different labour markets for different kinds of jobs.

Working in groups

Communication systems and effective 'downward communication' comes into this section. A reasonably straightforward question from a recent exam paper asked:

Why is it normally much easier to implement downward rather than upward systems for communication in an organisational hierarchy?

Unfortunately, candidates often run into problems with this type of question; the examiner's report referred to many answers which were 'depressingly weak, consisting of little more than pious generalities about the benefits of communicating in all directions, and offering little in the way of references to actual organisations or practical mechanisms for facilitating the communication process'.

Issues of power and control and the way managers 'get things done' frequently appear in exam questions. For example:

Using examples of both successful and unsuccessful attempts to 'get things done' in organisations, demonstrate the importance of understanding and exploiting what Weightman calls 'the subtleties of power', especially for people in the personnel function.

'Managing has been interpreted as controlling other people. This is a dangerously narrow view of the management process.' (Weightman.) Why? What in your opinion would be a more justifiable 'view' of the management process for today and the immediate future?

As you would expect in this section, the issue of working in groups and how to bring out the best in people is a likely question, for example:

In what circumstances are groups at work a 'good' thing or a 'bad' thing from the standpoint of the manager? Using your own organisation as an example, what positive steps can be taken by a manager to encourage 'good' group situations and discourage 'bad' ones?

Managing people in organisations

There is always a question which relates to the process of interviewing; however, the focus of the question can be either dealing with the poor performer, the selection interview or the appraisal interview, so it is not possible to 'question spot' with any accuracy.

Questions on the selection interview are often concerned with the precautions which can be taken to make 'failure' less likely, or place the interview in the context of the selection procedure as a whole, for example:

> Committed advocates of the one-to-one (selection) interview are often confronted by equally vociferous enthusiasts for the panel interview. What are the advantages and disadvantages of each, for both interviewer(s) and candidates? How could you devise a selection procedure which combines the benefits of both approaches?

The handling of disciplinary and counselling situations features regularly with such questions as:

> How could your organisation derive benefit from the behavioural sciences when setting up formal policies and practices for counselling employees with personal or performance difficulties?

Questions on appraisal will ask you to consider the effective design and operation of appraisal systems and how to overcome the pitfalls, for example:

> 'Performance appraisal is a waste of time if it consists principally of an assessment of performance over the past twelve months.' Discuss.

The systemic training process, and effective training methods to develop employees, are another area of the syllabus which tends to feature regularly, for example:

> Imagine that you have been asked to advise on the most effective training methods to be used for developing competent staff in any TWO categories:
> – Drivers of heavy goods vehicles delivering products to customers

- Sales representatives for a large insurance company
- Word processor operators
- Graduate management trainees.

Which training methods would you recommend in each of your two chosen cases, and why? How would you evaluate whether the training had been effective?

With reference to this last question, the examiner's report pointed out that many candidates were 'under the impression that "training" equals "courses". Few seemed to be aware of the increasing trend towards self-managed learning in its various forms, an approach certainly applicable to graduate management trainees and sales representatives. The other criticism concerns a lack of understanding about what is meant by "evaluation" in a training context.'

Motivation and incentives come into this part of the syllabus, but you will usually find that questions ask for the practical implications of the theories, or their relevance to effective organisational strategies for maximising employee performance. A typical question would be:

Examine the practical implications for managers of any TWO of the following 'theories':
- Maslow's Hierarchy of Needs
- Herzberg's Motivation-Hygiene Theory
- McGregor's Theory X and Theory Y
- Expectancy Theory

This question demands attention to practice and an answer would not gain good marks if it merely outlined two of the theories and did not demonstrate how they could be applied, had been perceived already in action, or could be refuted. Unquestioning regurgitation of Maslow's theory without alluding to its limitations (ethnocentric bias and neglect of spiritual issues, for example) would not be acceptable. Similarly Herzberg's and others' theories need to be put into the current context of recession, where managers are less interested in creating opportunities for job fulfilment than in the creation and maintenance of the jobs themselves.

Types of questions

The questions on this paper usually demand thought and interpretation and are framed in a way which requires you to carry out a critical analysis or develop an argument or justification for a course of action. There will usually be several parts to a question. If one part asks for a descriptive answer, a second part is most likely to require some analysis or argument, and more marks are likely to be awarded to the analysis part than to the description.

Questions will often involve you stating your own opinion or reflecting your values in your answers. You should not be afraid of doing this but it is important to support your ideas with facts, analysis and argument, rather than just present your view or values as an end in themselves. For example, in answering the performance appraisal question illustrated above, you might want to state what performance appraisal should consist of. But you need to give some explanation or justification for your views, as there is rarely one approach which is right in all situations.

Another type of dogmatic statement which should be avoided is unquestioning adherence to or acceptance of 'the way things are done' in your employing organisation. The examiner's report cites the example of the panel interview in public sector organisations, which candidates often do not evaluate against other selection procedures used in other organisations.

The questions are usually framed as essay-type questions, asking you to actually examine or discuss a proposition, define a concept and analyse its application, or compare and contrast two different views or approaches. You will therefore find the guidance in Chapters 6 and 9 on tackling essay-type questions of assistance with the Managing Human Resources examination paper.

Management Information Systems

The Management Information Systems module aims to give you an understanding of the information requirements of an organisation and how this information can be used to inform decision-making. On completion of the module you should be able to design a simple management information system, create a simple database, apply statistical techniques to problems, and use basic costing, budgeting and accounting principles for the purposes of planning and control.

The emphasis is on a basic level of competence. It is not expected that you will be taken through the detailed procedures of accounting and finance or sophisticated statistical approaches. Rather, a grounding in the principles and concepts and the development of a range of operational skills is intended. The course aims to provide an understanding of the typical processes undertaken by organisations in order to transform data into information for decision-making in various managerial functions. The learning from this module will be relevant to other modules in the PMFP and will be built upon at Stage 2, when, for example, you study human resource planning and compensation and benefits.

There will be both qualitative and quantitative questions and you will not be able to achieve a pass without attempting some quantitative questions.

Syllabus topics

The syllabus is divided into three sections, and there are usually four questions on the first section, and three questions on each of the other sections, although sometimes a question can span more than one section. Candidates are required to answer one question from each of the three sections and then a fourth question from the section of their choice. Usually a majority of candidates choose their fourth question from the first section, which has a qualitative rather than a quantitative focus.

Systems

Identifying the purpose and main characteristics of an information system usually appears as one part of a wider question. Typical questions would be:

> Explain the purpose of the information systems to be found at different organisational levels and identify their main distinguishing characteristics.

Outline the main characteristics of a management information system and who should determine them. How are these characteristics incorporated into the design and development of such a system?

What in your opinion are the main objectives of a management information system? How are they determined and incorporated into the system's design and development?

In the second and third example, you will see that the design and development of a system are involved. Such questions come up frequently, and may also be phrased as follows:

Discuss the process you would follow in carrying out the design or redesign of information systems for your organisation.

There are also a number of factors such as the 'people aspect' which should be taken into account, and a typical question is:

Discuss the constraints that managers need to take into account in the design of information systems to support financial decision-making.

There is also the issue of whether systems should be manual or computerised, and typical questions would be:

In what circumstances would you not recommend the use of computers for processing data and producing management information? Justify your view.

What options should be considered, and why, if you wanted to convert your personnel information system from a manual to a computer based system?

More general questions will ask you to discuss the scope for the use of information technology in operational and managerial control.

Identify the scope for the application of computers for operational and managerial control in your organisation.

Information technology's main role in an organisation is for the control of processes, money, people and materials. Elaborate this view and discuss its validity.

Statistics

The questions in the section on statistics will usually ask you to apply appropriate statistical techniques to a set of figures. Often it will be important for you to recognise the type of problem contained in the question so that you can select the most appropriate technique (see the first example question below). In addition, you may be asked to draw a graph or 'Z' chart showing trends or draw and explain the use of Lorenz curves. It will usually be necessary to briefly explain or comment upon your results.

Statistical techniques which often feature are the mean and standard deviation, also calculating the correlation coefficient and regression for a set of statistics. Typical questions are as follows:

An analysis of length of service of employees whose service has terminated produced the following data:

	Length of Service			
Entry Age	Less than 4 weeks	4–26 weeks	27–52 weeks	More than 52 weeks
Under 25	50	28	26	20
25 and under 35	20	32	50	30
35 and under 50	12	40	36	18
50 and under 65	16	31	27	22

You have been asked to analyse these figures to determine whether or not entry age has any bearing on length of service.

The time for entering data on a computer terminal is thought to be proportional to the number of entries made and a fixed time independent of this for selecting the source document, checking figures and other individual activity. The following times were logged for a sample of data entry tasks:

Time (mins)	No of entries
7.2	8
9.6	12
5.8	7
7.2	9
10.3	14
8.8	12
6.3	7
8.9	11
5.7	5
10.3	15
5.2	4
11.2	16

Calculate a regression formula for time taken on the number of entries and the correlation coefficient. Write a brief report on whether or not the regression formula could reliably be used to estimate the job content of a terminal operator.

British Atlantic Airways plc is evaluating two new aircraft for its fleet. These aircraft will be used on its exclusive service to Bangor International Airport (Maine, USA). Data gathered from the tests of the Federal Aviation Authority are shown below:

TRANSATLANTIC FLIGHT TIMES
(EXPECTED TIME 5 HOURS)

McDonald CB (hours)	Boderek 10 (hours)
4.81	4.88
5.07	5.04
5.13	5.11
4.78	5.27
5.27	4.83
5.51	5.06
4.86	5.03
4.89	4.79
5.35	5.05
5.03	4.87
5.01	5.26

The two aircraft appear to be identical in all other respects, such as operating costs, passenger capacity and reliability. The airline has therefore decided to select on the basis of flight times.

  (a) Calculate the mean deviation of flight times for the two aircraft;
  (b) Calculate the standard deviation of flight times for the two aircraft;
  (c) Comment on the results that you have obtained.

To answer such questions, it is essential to consider the type of problem involved and then to apply an appropriate technique. According to the examiner's report:

> Most candidates adopted a simplistic approach, using histo-grams, averages, cumulative frequencies, and did not recognise the opportunity for carrying out a chi-squared test for indepen-dence. The simplistic approaches frequently took up a lot of examination time . . .

Finance

To be able to answer questions in this section, you should be familiar with basic techniques for recording and presenting financial information. For example, you should be able to prepare a profit and loss account and a balance sheet and interpret the figures to assess the financial performance of a company. A typical question would be:

> Norma Bell plans to set up a business and informs you that her plans for the first six months of trading for the period 1st January to 30th June 1991 are as follows:
>
> a) Bell will put £15,000 into the business bank account on 1st January.
>
> b) Sales, all on credit, are expected to be:

January	£14,000	April	£24,000
February	18,000	May	16,000
March	20,000	June	18,000

Debtors will pay their accounts in the second month after that in which sales are made (i.e. January sales paid for in March).

c) Purchases, all on credit, will be:

January	£26,000	April	£21,000
February	17,000	May	14,000
March	19,000	June	11,000

Creditors will be paid in the month following that in which the goods are bought.

d) Wages and Salaries will be £850 per month payable on the last day of each month.

e) Drawings by the proprietor will be £1,000 per month payable on the last day of each month.

f) Premises costing £10,000 will be occupied on 1st January 1991, and will be paid for in February 1991.

g) All other expenses of £550 per month for the first five months and £800 for June are to be paid in the month following that in which they are incurred.

h) Equipment will be bought on 1st January 1991, for £2,000, payment being made in equal instalments in March and June.

i) Stock at 30th June 1991 will be £21,800.

j) Depreciation is to be written off the equipment at the rate of 20% per annum.

Required:
i) Draft a cash budget, showing clearly the bank balance or overdraft at the end of each month.

ii) Prepare a forecast Trading and Profit and Loss Account for the six months ended 30th June 1991 and a Balance Sheet at that date.

The question also involves preparing a cash budget, which is a regular feature of exam questions.

Other topics which come up are calculation of break-even and questions on key ratios. For example:

i) Discuss the concept of marginal costing and its usefulness for managerial decision-making.

ii) Fixed costs for a particular product are £100,000, the variable costs are £18 per unit and the selling price is £38.00. Draw a break-even chart for these figures and calculate the break-even point. If the maximum production is 7,000 units, what is the minimum price that the product could be sold for, if the target profit : fixed costs ratio required by the company is 0.15?

Define the key financial and performance ratios and discuss their use in the interpretation of accounts and the evaluation of managerial and organisation performance.

i) Explain briefly what ratios can be used to analyse accounts and what information they provide.

ii) The balance sheet for CRS plc is shown below:

	£,000		£,000	
	1989		1990	
Fixed Assets				
Land and Buildings		750		900
Plant and Machinery		750		800
Fixtures and Fittings		100		200
		1600		1900
Current Assets				
Stocks		500		600
Debtors		450		600
Cash		350		400
		1300		1600
Creditors (less than 1 year)				
Overdraft	180		200	
Trade Creditors	250		300	
		430		500
Net current Assets		870		1100

Total Assets less current liabilities	2470	3000
Creditors (over 1 year) Debentures	770	1000

Capital and Reserves				
Issued Share Capital	800		1000	
Reserves	900		1000	
Shareholders Interest		1700		2000
Total Long-term Capital		2470		3000

Calculate ratios and compare performances for 1989 and 1990 in the areas of liquidity, working capital, gearing and profitability.

Types of questions

The majority of questions on the Management Information Systems paper will require you both to demonstrate an understanding of concepts and principles by explaining or discussing your proposals or arguments, and to carry out calculations. Questions will often be made up of two or more sub-tasks and to gain good marks you are required to address each part of the question.

In quantitative questions, you should lay out your answers clearly and not adopt a 'back of an envelope' style. The logic underlying any computation must be shown. Although obtaining the correct answer is important, it is also required to show the method you have used. If the examiner can see the method you have used but you have made a minor error in calculation, you will not usually be heavily penalised. Credit is given to students who work out their answers rather than use a calculator. If calculations are relatively straightforward and merely involve the application of a formula, more weight will be placed on your comments and conclusions. The examiner will be looking here for calculation of correct results and then a commentary which indicates your understanding of concepts.

In questions with a more qualitative element, the approach to essay-type questions outlined in Chapters 6 and 9 will be more appropriate. The format of questions in Section A is largely of an essay type, with questions asking you to 'discuss' or 'explain'. Examples from your own experience or organisation should be used to illustrate your answers.

Questions in Sections B and C usually require you to calculate, although you may also be required to draw a chart or prepare a budget. In addition to the calculation you will usually be asked to comment briefly on your findings. This may take the form of an instruction to discuss the implications of the figures and the conclusions you draw from them, or you may be asked to write a brief report on your findings. In the time available in the exam you will probably be able to write no more than one or two paragraphs.

Where you present information in the form of charts or diagrams, you should not repeat verbally what is already clear enough in the diagram. Also, you should consider carefully what you are trying to convey in the diagram. The examiner has commented that diagrams often contribute little to the answers because they convey either too much information, or have insufficient annotation.

Chapter 12

Employee resourcing

At Stage 2 there are three principal subject areas, one of which is Employee Resourcing. The subject is divided between the compulsory core programme and a generalist module which may be replaced by a specialist module if you choose. For the purposes of this chapter, both the core and generalist modules will be considered together, but it will be made clear if a topic is not relevant to students following the specialist programme.

Taken together, the two Employee Resourcing modules account for 120 hours of tuition and so represent about three times the amount of effort required for a PMFP module. As a result it is more difficult to 'question spot' and you really need to learn broad topics so that you can apply your knowledge and understanding to a range of scenarios. It is not advisable to prepare for the exam on the basis of previous examination papers and examiners' reports. Rather you should base your preparation on the syllabus. Although there have not been major changes in the syllabus, it has been changed slightly several times recently, to reflect the constantly evolving context in which employee resourcing is conducted.

There has, of course, been the incorporation of an international dimension in the syllabus. Not only is there the influence of the European Community, but students also need to be aware of the effects of east and central Europe on the EC's labour markets, the significance of foreign companies operating in the UK, and the effects of development in the Pacific Basin on employment in Britain. There has also been increasing emphasis on the role of computers in personnel management and it is likely that each of the Stage 2 exam papers will include an IT-related question, which may or may not be part of the compulsory integrated question. Performance-related pay has been a preoccupation in many organisations in recent years and this has been reflected in both the syllabuses and exam papers.

In the view of the Chief Examiner, some of the most interesting issues facing personnel managers come up in the employee resourcing syllabus, and many of these are philosophical in nature. For example, what is meant by the term human resource management? When we pay people, are we compensating them for having to work or rewarding them for doing so? In order to reflect on such issues, you have to read widely to gain a breadth of knowledge, rather than just rely on lecture notes and practical skills and experience gained at work.

Wide reading also helps you to look beyond your own organisation and draw comparisons with the way things are done elsewhere. The Chief Examiner always tries to include questions about how practice can vary in different situations. He believes that there is no absolutely right way of doing things. To be successful in the Employee Resourcing examination, you need to develop a broad understanding of the issues raised by the syllabus. It is, however, possible to target your examination preparation and we will look at particularly important areas of the syllabus below.

Syllabus Topics

A study of the syllabus for Employee Resourcing 1 and 2 shows that, in addition to the topic of 'Modern Personnel Management', there are four sections in each module. In preparing the exam paper, the Chief Examiner seeks to align questions with these sections. Along with the first, compulsory question, and a last question, often on a general or topical issue, you will usually find questions on the sections as follows:

Core modules

Modern personnel management	
Human resource planning and organisation structure	1 or 2 questions
Employment	1 or 2 questions
Pay and employment conditions	1 question

Generalist module

Work organisation and human resource planning	1 question

Employment Pay and employment conditions	2 questions

Core and generalist module

Health, safety and welfare	1 question

For the purposes of study and revision, you will find it more helpful to divide up the syllabuses into topics. Within each topic area there will be an identifiable group of theories or concepts which pull together different strands and a range of possible 'angles' which the Chief Examiner could focus on in any particular diet of exams. What constitutes a 'topic' will depend partly on your own interests and partly on issues currently receiving the attention of your tutors and journal articles. However, the following list of 18 topics represents one way (my own particular analysis) of picking out essential areas of the syllabus from which to decide those you will concentrate on for revision purposes.

- Personnel management and HRM
- Computerised personnel information systems
- Flexible patterns of working and terms and conditions of employment
- Human resource planning including sources of information and methods of planning and control
- Organisation structure and culture and link to strategy
- Organisational and interpersonal communication
- Job design and team work
- Recruitment and selection strategy and methods
- Recruitment and selection agencies and consultants
- Performance appraisal schemes
- Discipline and dismissal, including exit interviews
- Equal opportunities legislation, policies and monitoring
- International employment, recruitment and compensation
- Payment schemes including job evaluation

- Pensions
- Incentive pay, especially performance-related pay
- Compensation packages
- Health and safety legislation and roles and safe working practices

We will now look briefly at each of these topics.

Personnel management and HRM

The contrast between HRM and personnel management does not feature regularly in the exam paper; rather, there is likely to be a more general question which requires you to refer to different patterns of personnel management and/or the relationship between personnel managers and other managers. So, for example, a recent question of a topical nature was:

> How is the nature of the personnel contribution different in times of economic recession than in times of economic growth?

Other questions have looked at how social and political changes in Europe are altering the scope of the work of British personnel managers, for example:

> How will the personnel contribution in British organisations change with the development of the European Community?

To be fully prepared on this aspect of the syllabus, you should understand the difference between the human resources approach and personnel management, and be able to give examples of any change in emphasis or direction for the personnel function in your own or other organisations.

Computerised personnel information systems

As we said above, there has been increasing interest in the role of computers in personnel management decision-making. As well as the development of 'hands-on' database skills through classroom exercises and assignments, you can expect an IT-related exam question to come up regularly. This may be as part of the compulsory integrated question – for example, the question analysed in Chapter 7. Whether in this form, or stand-alone, the following is a good example of the likely focus of a question:

> How, if at all, has the computer improved human resources management in the last five years? Provide practical examples in support of your answer.

According to the examiner's report, this question was generally well answered, with 'clear signs that the computer is at long last getting beyond the stage of being something nasty in the woodshed not to be touched with a bargepole by decent, clean-living personnel people. The best answers talked about how personnel can develop a much enhanced personnel service to the rest of the organisation and enhance the credibility of the personnel function in the process.'

Flexible patterns of working and terms and conditions of employment

The ideas of core and peripheral workforces and new patterns of working, such as annual hours contracts, home-working and self-employment, are resulting in a range of employment arrangements. To be prepared on this aspect of the syllabus you should be able to answer the following question:

> What do you understand by the terms 'core' and 'peripheral' workforces? In your organisation (or one with which you are familiar) how would you make this type of division and what would be the implications for personnel management?

A recent exam question along the same lines asked for the advantages to employers and individuals of resigning their contracts of employment and becoming self-employed, and an estimate of the scope for the wider application of this approach to employment.

Human resource planning

The topic of human resource planning includes sources of information within the organisation as well as external labour market data, and reconciling supply and demand to produce human resource plans which will meet business objectives. You could get a question on the type and use of information, methods of demand and supply forecasting, or the relationship between human resource plans and corporate plans. For example:

> What types of information about labour market trends are regularly available? How can this information be used in personnel management?

> Give examples of demand forecasting methods in manpower planning and explain how demand and supply forecasts can be reconciled.

> If an organisation is seeking to increase the customer-orientation of the business, what are the human resource issues in such an initiative, and how would they be incorporated in the human resource plan?

On this final question, the examiner's report comments:

> The best answers identified the central significance of attitudinal change and went on to describe how this might be tackled. Very few, however, mentioned some of the potential problems of such a programme, such as what to do about those who were uncooperative and how to control the costs. Some of the less successful answers merely described TQM or BS 5750.

Organisation structure and culture, and link with strategy

This topic builds on your studies at PMFP level and is likely to feature as part of a compulsory integrated question, as well as in specific questions drawing especially on the Employee Resourcing generalist module. A relatively straightforward recent exam question was:

> What is the role of the personnel function in developing:
> a) the organisation's culture, and
> b) the organisation's corporate strategy?

The external examiner's report indicates that students are more at ease with the topic of strategy than with the concept of culture. (One came up with a novel definition of the latter: 'Anything we do but monkeys don't.') A good answer would show a connection between the two, and give practical examples.

Organisational and interpersonal communication

The external examiner's report indicates that organisational communication is not an easy topic for students. He suggests that this may have something to do with personnel people losing the responsibility to the public relations function. A recent question in this area was:

> *How can the effectiveness of organisational communication be monitored?*

Job design and team work

This topic is in the Employee Resourcing generalist module and would only need to be studied if you were taking that module.

The syllabus could be divided into two topics if you prefer, but it has been combined here because job redesign often involves building in opportunities for individuals to work together in teams. A recent question was:

> How can the activities of groups and individuals in your organisation be integrated and co-ordinated without limiting necessary freedom of action and autonomy? Provide practical examples in support of your answer.

This is seeking practical examples and provides a particular 'angle' which should be addressed. A straightforward description of job design theories or motivation is not likely to lead to a pass mark.

Recruitment and selection strategy and methods

There is usually a question on some aspect of recruitment and selection on the exam paper, but it could be on overall strategy, methods of selection, or the use of agencies and consultants (discussed under the next point). For revision purposes you will need to be familiar with the range of methods and their advantages and disadvantages, as you could be required to comment generally on the methods to use in a specific situation, or asked for your views on one particular method. For example:

> How can you evaluate the effectiveness of your methods of recruitment and selection?

Unfortunately, recruitment and selection tends to be one of those questions where candidates see a 'green light' and don't make the best use of their knowledge by applying it to the specific question being asked. According to the examiner's report a typical error is to answer the question as if it were simply asking: 'How do you carry out recruitment and selection where you work?' or 'What does a good recruitment and selection process look like?' Instead, candidates should answer the question by adding the following points to their description of recruitment and selection methods:

- To evaluate the success of your system of recruitment and selection, you need to work out what the success criteria are. These will be related to the needs of the business, in its current and future situation.
- The measures of evaluation need to be described and justified. These could include turnover/wastage rates, exit interviews, performance appraisal, the level of incidents such as disciplinary or grievance cases, accidents, sickness, response to advertising, the cost per applicant, equal opportunities monitoring, and so forth. As well as mentioning the measures, you need to highlight which ones will be appropriate for the specific success criteria you have set out and to show the link between the criteria and the measures. The measure of overwhelming importance in evaluating effectiveness is likely to be job performance.

An example of a question on a particular method is:

> In what circumstances, and why, would you use psychological testing as part of the selection process?

The key points to note in this question are that you are required to (i) indicate a range of circumstances such as in general screening, or within assessment centres, and (ii) say why, for example for greater objectivity.

Recruitment and selection agencies and consultants

The use of external agencies for recruitment and selection comes up in the Employee Resourcing generalist syllabus (see below), and so can be treated as a separate topic. A typical question would be:

> From the standpoint of your own organisation, in what circumstances and how would you use each of the following:
> a) A recruitment advertising agency
> b) A Job Centre
> c) Executive search?

Again, the key point is to answer that part of the question concerned with 'how', as well as describing the circumstances.

Performance appraisal schemes

Performance appraisal interviewing and the design of an appraisal scheme are included in the Managing Human Resources module of the PMFP, therefore you are likely to get a question which is more demanding, as opposed to straightforward. A recent question concerned the problems with appraisal and asked how these would be overcome in organisations:

> In 1989 the American management consultant Tom Peters described performance appraisal as 'the number one American management problem . . . it takes the average employee (manager or non-manager) six months to recover from it.' To what extent is that true in your organisation? If true, how could the problems be reduced; if not true, how have the problems been avoided?

This topic is a good one to revise as it also features on the Employee Development syllabus.

Discipline and dismissal

Discipline, dismissal and exit interviews come up regularly on the exam paper and like appraisal, this is a good topic to revise as disciplinary issues also feature on the Employee Relations syllabus. The topic features in both the Employee Resourcing core and generalist modules, and is often a popular choice of question, but the following example will indicate the need to answer the question, and not just write what you know:

> Describe and justify your view of a constructive approach to discipline at work.

The first part of the answer will involve a description of 'constructive approach to discipline'. It is not adequate to simply describe a disciplinary procedure, for example that suggested by ACAS, which advocates a wider approach. The second part of the question will require you to 'justify' what you have described.

A good answer will take a broad view of discipline, including self-discipline, as a means towards effective individual and organisational performance, rather than just a necessary administrative preliminary to dismissal. If you describe the procedure which operates at your own place of work, remember to critically assess it and justify why you think it is constructive.

On the subject of exit interviews, the following is an example of a recent question:

> When members of your organisation leave, what are the advantages of conducting a leaving interview? How should the interview be carried out in order to achieve the benefits you have described?

Again, a two-part question. As well as asking for advantages, the second part of the question asks 'how' to carry out an interview. Some of the points to be included would be:

- Conduct the interview away from the workplace
- Interview carried out by personnel people, not line
- Guarantee confidentiality and that references will not be affected

- Obtain union agreement to the process if unions are recognised
- Probe into interviewee's responses for the factors 'pushing' as well as 'pulling'.

Equal opportunities

Equal opportunities legislation, and the design and monitoring of policies, are in the Employee Resourcing generalist module, although the legal aspects will come into the core module too. A question could concern overall policies, or methods of monitoring, as the following two examples indicate:

> 'Equalising employment opportunity is not in the management interest.' Set out the arguments for *and* against that proposition.

> Review the methods of monitoring equality of employment opportunity in your organisation. How do you think they could be improved?

Many students, according to the examiner's report, failed to produce a balanced response to the first question:

> Most seemed quite incapable of seeing any arguments at all to support the proposition. Because of this, their arguments against it were seldom cogent. Better answers considered with some care what 'the management interest' actually was before considering the for and against arguments. There was also a tendency to discuss equal opportunities in terms of improving opportunities for women, occasionally extended to include the minority ethnic populations and, even more occasionally, the differently abled.

International employment

Expatriate and international employment, recruitment issues and forms of employment package come into the Employee Resourcing generalist module and are also the subject of a module for continuous professional development on completion of the Professional Education Scheme. This topic does not feature regularly in the exam paper.

Payment schemes including job evaluation

There is often a question on the exam paper relating to an aspect of compensation. This could be on payment schemes, pensions, performance-related pay or other benefits. We have divided this area up into four related topics and give examples of typical questions under each, firstly on payment schemes:

> In what ways are employer objectives for payment schemes different from employee objectives, and in what ways are they the same?

The examiner's report indicates that students found it easier to discuss employer objectives, including attraction, retention, image, culture, quality, output and control, than employee objectives. In this type of question, you can refer to motivation theories as an example of underpinning knowledge.

Pensions

The topic of pensions is contained in the Employee Resourcing core module and it features occasionally on exam papers. A typical question would be:

> What advice about pension arrangements would you give to employees who are about to become self-employed?

Incentive pay

Incentive pay, and performance-related pay in particular, comes up regularly on exam papers, sometimes as part of the compulsory integrated question, as in the example in Chapter 7. Another typical question would be:

> How do you measure the effect on performance of performance-related pay schemes?

This question requires you to consider the type of PRP that can be used, the aims, the criteria that are used for performance and the approach to using the criteria.

Compensation packages

Remuneration packages and benefits feature in the Employee Resourcing generalist module, and are only occasionally found on the exam paper, but a recent example was as follows:

> Describe and justify the arrangements you use, or would use, for dealing with the following:
> a) Company cars and/or mileage allowances,
> and
> b) *Subsistence and other travelling expenses.*

As with many questions of this type, individual candidates were better on the description than on the justification. For a good mark, you need to address both parts of the question.

Health and safety

Health and safety features in both the core and generalist modules and there is usually a question on some aspect of the topic. Changes to legislation to make it more effective, managing health and safety and the coordination of roles and responsibilities are more usually the subject of questions, but occasionally there may be one on hazards and safe working practices. The examiners' reports indicate that health and safety questions are not particularly popular, which is surprising since they are so regularly featured. Examples include:

> What changes would you make in the work-related health and safety legislation of the United Kingdom? What would be the effect of these changes on your organisation?

> How can the activities of personnel staff, safety officers and occupational health professionals in the organisation be coordinated to ensure both effectiveness and observance of differing codes of professional ethics?

The former question, according to the examiner's report, was often used by candidates solely 'to show off how much fine detail was known about current legislation, including the precise dates of statutes and substantial word-for-word extracts from it'. Others fell into a common trap and 'answered a question which was *not* asked: "What impact will Europe have on health and safety legislation in the UK?" '

In the latter question, it would be possible to describe the framework of responsibilities in your own organisation and then go on to consider the conflicts which arise between differing codes of professional ethics. For example, there is the issue of confidentiality of medical records, and production targets being threatened because of safety problems.

In revising, concentrate on general issues rather than on learning all the dates of the legislation. It is more important to be able to place legislation in its historical context than to write out details.

Types of Questions

The questions in the Employee Resourcing examination paper require you to be able to apply what you have learned to situations. Sometimes the organisation in which you work or another with which you are familiar is referred to, and sometimes a specific situation is given. There are no questions which simply ask you to describe a technique or process, for example job evaluation or human resource planning, although a brief description is usually one element of an answer. In addition, you will normally be asked to analyse a situation, summarise and criticise the different viewpoints, and present a persuasive argument.

Personal experience and practical examples are always helpful in answers; however, good marks will not be gained if you give an uncritical account of how things are done within one organisation. The answers should show that you see yourself as part of management and can propose realistic solutions, bearing in mind constraints which may be operating. Solutions should be justified, for example if you suggest holding a meeting, you should indicate the purpose of the activity you are proposing.

The Chief Examiner repeatedly points out that you must answer the question and not waste time displaying knowledge you happen to have which is not relevant to the set question. A common fault with poorer answers is that they pick out and deal with only the easy bits, but leave out the trickier bits. The following example shows how to deal with a typical question on this paper.

From the standpoint of your own organisation, in what circumstances and how would you use each of the following:
a) A recruitment advertising agency
b) A Job Centre
c) Executive search?

The points to bear in mind in answering this question are:

- 'Your own organisation' means you should answer from the perspective of the organisation in which you work.
- 'In what circumstances' could include business aspects like unexpected expansion, a shortage of staff in the personnel department, a desire to prevent competitors knowing of a particular appointment, or the need to approach a specific individual. It is not just asking 'for what jobs'.
- 'How would you' requires that you justify the action you propose, and is different to the question 'how does your organisation'. So, for example, you may answer that you would use a Job Centre for unskilled or seasonal staff for reasons of cost effectiveness, or because selection criteria are unimportant.
- 'Each' means that you have to address all three parts of the question. If however you would not use one or all of the examples, you can answer in that way, provided you explain why.

Most questions are framed as essay-type questions and usually have at least two parts which have to be answered. The guidance in Chapters 6 and 9 on tackling essay-type questions will be useful to you. Occasionally a question may demand a different form of presentation. For example:

How could matters relating to employee health and safety be managed better where you work? Present your answer in a way that would convince the Chief Executive.

The question asks for a convincing presentation, which means that you would set out your answer as a report or a memo, or, more innovatively, as a face-to-face presentation. Whichever you choose, you should make it clear what the method of presentation is to be.

Chapter 13

Employee development

The syllabus comprises both the 'core' and 'generalist' modules of Employee Development. Topic headings in the generalist module largely repeat those in Employee Development 1, but Employee Development 2 is a more complex and detailed treatment of the subject areas. For the purpose of this chapter, both the core and generalist modules will be considered together, but it will be made clear if a topic is not relevant to students who have decided to follow a specialist module rather than Employee Development 2.

As with the other Stage 2 subjects, Employee Development accounts for 120 hours of tuition. It builds on topics covered in the PMFP, particularly learning theory and the approaches to training and development covered in the Managing Human Resources module.

There have not been any major changes in the syllabus recently, but the emphasis of exam questions has been gradually evolving to reflect changes in the external environment and new approaches and issues in employee development. There have been, for example, changes in national institutions and policies in education and training; comparisons with European approaches have informed British initiatives; and the development of advanced training methods such as CBT (computer based training). It is not advisable therefore to prepare for the exam on the basis of 'question-spotting' in previous exam papers. Rather, you should ensure that you have studied and revised key areas of the syllabus.

The Chief Examiner for the Employee Development paper is looking for a strong practical focus in the answers to questions. An aspect which is particularly emphasised is the need for a realistic understanding of costs and the financial implications of proposals. Answers must reflect an appreciation of practical, commercial considerations and proposals must be appropriate for the context.

From May 1994, the exam paper will be divided into three

sections. Section A will continue to be a compulsory integrated question. Section B will relate primarily to national policy and practice and the role of training and development in the organisation. Section C will mainly concern the training and development process and specific issues and approaches. You will be required to answer at least one question from Section B and C plus one other, in addition to the compulsory question.

Syllabus Topics

There are four main areas to the syllabuses for Employee Development 1 and 2. You can always expect at least one question covering national policy and practice, the role of training and development in organisations, identifying training needs and designing training programmes, and specific issues and approaches. However, questions do not usually fall neatly into one or other part of the syllabus. Typically a question will require you to draw on knowledge and skills from two parts. For example, a question on identifying training needs will not be posed in the abstract, so that you can just describe methods, but will usually relate to a particular category of employee or current issue, drawn from another area of the syllabus.

There is also a strong practical focus in the exam paper and you will need to be prepared to answer questions which require you to demonstrate your skills as a training practitioner. These questions might ask you to prepare a training plan or write a training programme.

For the purposes of study and revision, you will find it helpful to divide up the syllabuses into topics, but it is important that you do not compartmentalise your learning. As you learn how to design a training programme or learning event, consider how you apply this learning to a range of practical situations. Then you will not be 'put off your stride' in the examination if a scenario is presented with which you have no prior experience.

The following list of topics represents my analysis of the essential areas of the syllabus for study and revision purposes:

- National training institutions and initiatives
- International comparisons

- Learning and self-development
- Role of training and development in organisations
- Identifying training needs
- Training planning/programme design
- Methods of training
- Assessment of learning
- Specific approaches and issues.

We will now look briefly at each of these topics.

National training institutions and initiatives

The national scene is constantly evolving with new institutions and initiatives. You need to be up-to-date with the most recent developments in order to answer a question successfully. Reading personnel management and training publications as well as the quality press and watching out for documentaries on television should keep you in touch with the changing scene. Textbooks and lecture notes will provide you with an overview of the longer-term evolution of the institutions and national training framework. It is not necessary to learn the provisions of all the Acts of Parliament and white papers of the last 30 years, though you should be aware of their purposes and the circumstances they sought to deal with. In this way you will be able to put into context the more recent initiatives and critically assess their relevance, and likely success.

Recent national initiatives have included the following:

- Training and Enterprise Councils (LECs in Scotland)
- National Vocational Qualifications (NVQs)
- Investors in People
- National Training Awards
- National Training Targets

A typical question on this area of the syllabus would be:

Training and Enterprise Councils (TECs) [LECs in Scotland] have been designed primarily to work with local labour markets. Many employee development issues are national or specific to occupational groupings, e.g. managers or engineers.

To what extent and how can these different needs be reconciled?

The question requires an understanding of the purposes of TECs and their essentially local focus, in comparison with their predecessors in the training field, such as the Engineering Industry Training Board. The TECs' potential contribution to different development needs should be explained and the role of coordinating bodies and other agencies, such as TEED, MCI and NCVQ, in providing the rational overview.

International comparisons

International aspects of training and education are contained in the Employee Development generalist module syllabus.

Many of the recent developments in Vocational Education and Training (VET) arrangements have been influenced by international comparisons with countries in the European Community as well as Japan and the United States. The French Training Tax can be contrasted with the voluntary approach to investment in training in the UK. The 'Dual System' of Germany has been influential in a number of recent developments. For this part of the syllabus, you should have an overview of the strengths and weaknesses of different approaches used by such international competitors and be able to evaluate their usefulness or limitations for the British context. A typical question on this area of the syllabus would be:

> The 'dual system' for vocational training used in Germany features close collaboration between employers and employee representatives or trade unions. To what extent do you consider British arrangements for vocational training bring together employer and employee interests? What improvements would you recommend?

Learning and self-development

An understanding of learning and self-development is valuable in underpinning other areas of the syllabus, and you will also find specific questions on aspects of learning and self-development.

This is an area where there has been much recent research and new ideas are influencing the approaches to employee development. There has, for example, been research in both the UK and the United States on the 'learning organisation', and a move towards learner-centred approaches to employee development, as opposed to more traditional, directive forms of teaching and learning. The work of Kolb, and Honey and Mumford is relevant to this topic in helping to identify the range of learning opportunities you could use.

For this topic you need to understand the Continuous Professional Development (CPD) philosophy advocated by the IPM, how to create schemes for employee self-development, and how to implement a learner-centred approach to development in your organisation. You can also reflect on your own experience as an IPM student and how you made best use of learning opportunities available to you.

Typical questions on this area of the syllabus include:

> Recent research has indicated that in the future successful organisations of all types will need to be 'Learning Organisations' if they are to cope with the increasing complexities of the 21st century. Explain what the term 'Learning Organisation' means to you and identify at least SIX factors you would look for in such an organisation. Then, assess the degree to which your current organisation could be described as a learning organisation.

> Individuals are ultimately responsible for their own learning. What elements would you expect to see in an Employee Development Policy Statement designed to enable this? Justify your view.

The examiner's report sets out the problems some candidates had with the first of these two questions: 'The use of theoretical or academic reference material was disappointing. Many answers did not demonstrate the ability to apply theory in the context of actual organisations. The essential point of adaptability to the environment was often missed. The Learning Organisation concept was too often simply equated to Continuous Professional Development.'

Role of training and development in organisations

This part of the syllabus is concerned with understanding how the training and development function can be effective and prove its worth to the organisation. It can be studied from several angles. First of all, there have been changes in typical roles and responsibilities in recent years and you need to understand the different ways that training and development can contribute to business needs. Personnel specialists often have employee development responsibilities, and development roles are more likely to involve line managers, for example in coaching and mentoring. There have been moves in many organisations to make training a profit centre, and in others the cost of maintaining an in-house training centre has been evaluated. A realistic appreciation of costs clearly comes into this part of the syllabus.

In addition, we have recently had the results of the Training and Development Lead Body, which has set standards of competence for trainers, and the competence movement generally is being applied successively to all occupational areas. You therefore need to understand the influence of these national developments on training and development in organisations.

Occasionally, you will find questions on the exam paper which are concerned with the selection and training of training staff, for which you will need an understanding both of their roles in organisations, and of the skills of designing training programmes. Examples of questions on this part of the syllabus are:

> Training and development should be a profit centre just like any other business unit. What are your views for and against this proposition? On balance, do you agree or disagree?

> You have been asked to assess whether your organisation should continue to operate its 40-bedroomed training centre in the South East of England. The organisation has six divisional offices and 300 branch offices throughout the UK. The cost of running the centre is similar to using hotels to run the same volume of training. Specify clearly what criteria you would use to decide whether to keep the centre or sell it.

These questions are related to the Employee Development generalist module, but the compulsory integrated questions are likely to involve this topic too. The examiner's report comments on where students went wrong with the first of these questions:

> There was widespread misunderstanding of the term 'profit centre'. Too many answers failed to demonstrate the ability to marshal arguments and justify a view . . . There was a suggestion that public sector candidates may have found the question more difficult.

Identifying training needs

There are a range of methods for identifying training needs, employee performance and potential, and you need to be aware of them and their application in different contexts. However you are unlikely to get a question which only focuses on this aspect of the syllabus. Rather, you will need to apply your understanding to a specific issue or group of employees, and probably produce a training plan or programme. Therefore it is essential that you revise this aspect of the syllabus and bring in your knowledge where relevant to particular questions. An example of a question which will involve identifying training needs is as follows:

> You are planning to arrange a learning programme for 30 women who will take up their first managerial appointment over the next 6–12 months. They currently undertake a wide range of occupations within your organisation. How would you undertake this task? Identify what steps you would take, outline content and methods proposed for the programme and an approximate budget for the whole process.

This question, according to the examiner's report, revealed many candidates' lack of financial expertise:

> There is clearly a need to create more realism and under-standing in students' ideas on costs. Assumptions about facilities costing nothing because they were already there were indicative of this. There was some tendency to avoid the 'women's' issues and answer the question with a general introduction to management programmes.

Training planning/programme design

You can expect several questions on the exam paper which will require you to demonstrate your skills in preparing training plans and/or outlining a training programme. Here again, the question of costs is relevant, and you must show a realistic appreciation of the likely costs of the proposals you make. It is also important to link plans to business needs, as opposed to training for training's sake. Involving the client or learner in the design of training plans and programmes is essential if the solutions are to gain acceptance. Typical questions include:

> You have been asked to prepare a brief outline training plan for your organisation. In outline report format identify:
> – what occupation areas it would cover
> – what training and development methods would be used for each occupation
> – what approximate costs would be involved
> – what resources would be required
> – how Computer Based Training, Open Learning, Interactive Video and other non-traditional methods could contribute.

> Four managers from Eastern Europe will be visiting your organisation later in the year. They will be with you for six weeks. Prepare an outline programme designed to enable them to understand how your organisation operates in a 'free-market' economy. Specify what employee development methods will be used.

Where a question asks you to prepare an outline training programme, you should begin by specifying real, measurable learning objectives and outline the programme with a justification of the methods to be used. Frequently the question will require you to state how you will assess whether it has been successful, and of course, make reference to the costs involved.

The question above on Eastern European managers is an example of a scenario you might be presented with in the exam and your first reaction may be that you know nothing about Eastern Europe. The key point to remember is that you have acquired the skills of training programme design and can apply them to the range of possible scenarios which may feature on the exam paper.

Methods of training

The syllabus covers a number of methods of training which you should be familiar with so that you can recommend the most appropriate choice of methods for the scenario you are presented with. In recent years there has been a move to student-centred methods, and the widespread introduction of open and distance learning. Technology is also increasingly influencing methods of training and instruction, and you should be aware of the possible contribution of interactive video and CBT. You will note that in the question quoted above on training planning, the use of these non-traditional methods was included within the question. The Chief Examiner has indicated a concern at the level of awareness of CBT. A recent question which included reference to training methods and CBT is given below:

> You have been asked to design a two-day programme on project management for professional staff employed at 40 sites throughout the UK. A Computer Based Training (CBT) programme produced by the organisation on the topic is available. Draft a suitable approach to include programme content and methods proposed.

Students who are not studying the Employee Development generalist module would not cover advanced training methods.

Assessment of learning

Similarly, work-based assessment and accreditation come in the Employee Development generalist module. Typically the assessment of learning will come into other questions on the exam paper, but with recent developments in the use of work-based learning and the greater weighting given to assessing competence in the IPM's education scheme, this topic is likely to feature more regularly. A recent question was as follows:

A training log can provide a useful means of improving the assessment of continuous learning. What would you expect such a log to include and how would you measure progress? Use your own job or one you are familiar with to construct a specimen page.

Specific approaches

In the Employee Development generalist module the fourth part of the syllabus is entitled 'Specific Approaches and Issues in Training and Development'. This lists a number of rather unrelated topics and issues and in the time available in your programme of study, you couldn't cover all of them.

Your tutor will be able to indicate topical issues and your reading of personnel and training articles will help you to identify possible areas which might feature on the exam paper. There are however some training and development issues which you should be reasonably familiar with like equal opportunities and women's training and development, also career planning and management development. The Chief Examiner has indicated that he feels career management is a central aspect of employee development, and you should therefore ensure that you know how to plan and implement a career development programme. The following is a recent example of a question in this area:

Identify the main challenges to be met by a plan to identify and develop high-fliers to fill the top 100 key roles in a major organisation. The plan will take two years to launch and cover a 10-year period. Specify what types of measures of success you would use, e.g. two qualified successors available for each key job within five years.

Also, the question quoted under 'Identifying training needs' (page 182) is an example.

You can expect current issues and concerns to be featured in exam questions, for example handling change and organisational restructuring. Two recent examples of questions are:

Change has become a permanent condition for many organisations. Identify the four or five major changes that you anticipate will affect your organisation over the next two years. Outline the probable training and development requirements with a clear indication of programme content for two or three of the changes.

Your organisation has decided to eliminate one level of management. You have the responsibility to design a programme to help those staff who will be made redundant. These number 100 and range in age from 25 to 60 years. Identify the main elements of a programme to help individuals to cope with the change and to find new jobs. You have been allocated £25,000 for the task and should identify clearly what methods you would use.

Such questions require that you bring in your knowledge and skills from other areas of the syllabus in order to produce a satisfactory answer.

Type of Questions

The questions on the Employee Development exam paper are intended to offer opportunities for you to demonstrate conceptual awareness and an ability to operate in a practitioner and managerial role. Questions can take a variety of forms. You may be asked to recommend action in your 'own organisation' (or an organisation with which you are familiar), or a mini-case-type question may be included. Often questions will require a specified form of answer, such as:

• Prepare an outline training plan
• Prepare a draft training programme
• Construct a specimen page in a training log
• Draft a policy statement
• Draft a memo

Where the format is specified, marks will be awarded for using the form of presentation required and merely describing the contents will be unlikely to achieve a pass mark.

You must demonstrate that you are aware of what constitutes effective employee development action at the workplace. This means you must be familiar with the material in the syllabus and capable of applying it to analysis and argument. The questions will assume that you are at the level of training officer/manager in a small to medium-sized organisation, and not expect you to envisage yourself in a senior role in a large organisation. Therefore the level of understanding and application which is required is higher than can be gained from general reading.

Examiners will look to see if material is presented in a practical way. An answer which includes relevant examples of real-life practice will be valued, as will answers which clearly show that you can relate to commercial needs. The managerial focus which is required means that you should show a technical understanding of an issue, an appreciation of costs, and also a political awareness of the practicalities of gaining support for training and development solutions. This is distinct from a management view, which other managers in the organisation have and might want you to adopt.

A management style involves a willingness to take personal responsibility for the conclusions or recommendations you make. Answers should be persuasive, giving the reasons for your views or proposals. The examiner will accept an answer which disagrees with a statement, or differs from the expected answer, provided your reasoning is shown. Negative remarks not backed by remedial proposals will not be valued.

The Chief Examiner has commented that weaker answers do not demonstrate an ability to apply theory to practical situations or put ideas into a practical context. In the question on learning organisations on page 180 above, many students could explain the concept, but were not able to link it to the need for adaption to the business environment. Similarly, in questions on training plans, it is important to link plans to business needs. There needs to be a balance in your answers between theory and practice. Some questions do demand that you demonstrate an understanding of theories. In the following question, you would need to explain learning theories in the context of how people learn.

Identify and describe in detail which approaches to learning have worked best for you in your IPM studies. Why do you think those particular approaches were best for you? How would you advise new IPM students to maximise their learning opportunities?

The above question is also a good example of the type which is in several parts. There are three parts to this question and all must be addressed in order to gain a good mark. You will find that all questions on the exam paper are made up of two or more parts. In this instance, according to the examiner's report, 'few of the answers gave adequate coverage to the advice for new IPM students'. They also tended to stress only one view of learning: 'Considerable attention was given to Mumford and Honey on Learning Styles. One wonders if the theory was taken too literally and seen too much as normative rather than descriptive. Consideration of other aspects of learning was rather limited.'

As well as questions which require you to present your answer in a particular format, there are also questions which ask you to 'discuss', 'describe and justify', and give your views for and against a proposition. These can be tackled using the guidelines for essay-type questions which are given in Chapters 6 and 9. A typical example is given below:

Explain, with examples, the criteria you would apply in deciding whether to recommend the use of internal or external training resources. If external resources are used, what are the critical procedures needed to ensure that the training remains relevant to actual work needs?

An outline answer using the matrix approach has been prepared to show you how you might tackle it.

Introduction

  i) Definition of internal and external resources.
 ii) Summary of criteria which would be used.
iii) The sequence in which the question will be answered.

Main body

Part A: Criteria to use in deciding between internal and external resources

Analysis	Argument	
CRITERIA	INTERNAL	EXTERNAL
1. Objectives	Is practice in the work environment required?	Is contact with people outside the organisation required?
2. Transfer to work situation	Easier to do	Are there features to aid this?
3. Resources available and cost	Do we have the facilities, equipment, expertise?	Are there colleges or other suppliers available?
4. Trainee factors	Numbers and expectations	Will they be required to travel away from work/home?
5. Organisation policy and culture	Is internal preferred?	Will managers give release from work?

Examples must be given of the criteria. It may be that trainees must learn on the equipment on the supplier's premises. If trainees are to learn to clean production equipment, off-the-job instruction would not be sufficient. Expertise in psychological testing may not be available in-house, so expert resources external to the organisation must be employed. If there are large numbers requiring a particular type of training, it may be more cost-effective to train a training officer in the technique, then run in-house programmes. Some programmes, such as management development, need to be tailored to the organisation culture, and may need a mix of internal and external resources.

Part B: The critical procedures to ensure external resources remain relevant

Check supplier's experience, ability to fit the product to the learning objectives, and learning methods to be used.

Involve line managers in identifying needs and briefing trainees.

Provide mentoring and coaching.

Ensure managers undertake debriefing and follow up on application of learning through appraisal and review.

Periodically review provision to ensure that it remains up to date and relevant to work needs.

Conclusion

Sum up main ideas and arguments e.g. the importance of cost and training being relevant to business needs, and writing as the training officer, indicate the key procedures which you would implement.

Chapter 14

Employee relations

The subject of Employee Relations is covered in a 'core' and 'generalist' module. The topic headings in the syllabuses appear at first sight to be different, but in fact, on closer inspection you will find that the generalist module looks at similar topics in more depth than the core module. For the purposes of this chapter, both the modules will be considered together, and it will be made clear if the topic is not relevant to students who have decided not to follow the generalist module.

The Chief Examiner has recently updated the syllabus for the core module. The overall learning objectives remain the same, but the detailed content reflects the greater weighting given to the development of skills in both the Professional Education Scheme as a whole, and within the Employee Relations examination paper. There is now more emphasis on employee relations procedures and rather less on the purely legalistic aspects of the subject. The growing importance of Europe and of communication strategies in organisations, as well as changes in employee relations practice and public policy, have been incorporated into the syllabus and examination paper. Also, do not forget the point made in Chapter 12 that each of the Stage 2 exam papers is likely to include a question which relates in some way to information technology.

The Employee Relations paper is divided into three sections. Section A contains the compulsory integrated question. Section B concentrates on the wider context of the subject of employee relations and includes the institutions and processes of an employee relations system. In other words, it deals with the 'macro' aspects. Section C, by contrast, largely relates to the skills required by an employee relations manager. There are four questions in Section B and five questions in Section C, and you are required to answer one from each section plus a further question chosen from either section.

191

The employee relations skills part of the syllabus considers types of negotations and the skills required at various stages in the process of negotiations, for example strategic thinking, information gathering, planning, presentation and note-taking. This section also includes the skills and procedures required to handle other types of employee relations situations such as grievances, discipline, disputes and redundancy.

A mistaken view is the perception that employee relations are about dealing with trade unions and that if you work in a non-unionised environment, it is not relevant to you. Wherever there is an employment relationship, there is the potential for conflict over the price of labour. An appreciation of management objectives in engaging in employee relations activities, the ritual of bargaining, the skills involved in negotiating and problem solving, and the relevance of membership of employer organisations, are essential elements in the 'kit bag' of the personnel manager.

Syllabus Topics

For the purposes of study and revision, you will find it helpful to divide up the syllabus into topics which fall into either the 'macro' section or the 'skills' section of the exam paper. Although of course the underpinning principles and concepts are the same, the style of exam questions and coverage are different. Here, we will first look at the 'macro' topics and then the 'skills' topics.

Section B: Context, institutions and processes

The Chief Examiner sees employee relations as a process of resolving differences between the buyers and sellers of labour over 'price'. The different *interests* of the buyers and sellers are resolved by making *agreements* (of various types and varying formality), through the use of different *processes* (such as collective bargaining, joint consultation, third party intervention, participation). The outcome of this 'employee relations game' is highly influenced by the balance of *bargaining power* between the buyers and sellers of labour services, which in turn is determined by factors such as the level of economic activity and the legal framework, which are external to the workplace. Employee relations, then, is a game of reconciling interests, and depending on the balance of bargaining power at any one time, the way in which the game is played can change.

An analysis of the syllabus shows that issues like the context in which employee relations take place, the range of parties and institutions, and the processes used, are key areas. There is also the impact of the Single European Market on employee relations, policies and practices. We will therefore look at typical questions which fall under these headings; however, you should bear in mind that questions often combine aspects of the syllabus, for example the purposes of trade unions may be combined with employee relations processes. There is therefore a requirement to have a broad understanding of the syllabus, and it would not be advisable to try to 'question spot' and bank on a particularly favourite topic coming up.

Components of employee relations

The Chief Examiner's view is that the study of employee relations is 'the reconciliation of the interests of the buyers and sellers of labour services'. You will therefore find that a question asking you to discuss this view crops up periodically. To answer it you need to recognise that the buyers and sellers of labour services have a common interest in reconciling their different economic interests through making agreements by different employee relations processes. You also need to bring in the wider environmental context within which these processes are operating; economic, political, legal and technological factors will determine the balance of bargaining power. A recent question was:

> To what extent do collective relationships exist in non-unionised establishments or firms? Give examples to justify your answer.

The Chief Examiner's report on this question indicated that:

> Few students discussed or mentioned the 'conflict' between the buyers and sellers of labour. Some students mentioned staff associations but did not seem to appreciate the similarities between staff associations and trade unions. There was little discussion of the kinds of collective issues that can arise in non-unionised firms. There was too much uncritical presentation of a unitarist approach to employee relations. Exam-

ples of so-called unitarist firms were poor in that these companies would not deny conflict in industry, but merely choose to manage that conflict without unions.

Parties in employee relations

Questions about the parties in employee relations might ask you to discuss management strategies and approaches regarding trade unions, the role of employers' associations, or the organisation and functions of trade unions. Typical questions include:

> Some organisations manage their employee relations with their employees in trade unions but others prefer to do so with their employees outside trade unions. Explain, with examples
> a) why
> *and*
> b) how this takes place.

> What changes, and why, in the functions of employers' associations do you think will be necessary if they are to be influential on employee relations developments in the 1990s?

Some students, according to the examiner's report, answered the latter question badly because they 'demonstrated a woeful misunderstanding of the role of employers' associations. They relied on applying the findings of the Donovan Report (1968) to the challenges facing such associations in the 1990s.' Knowledge of the function of state agencies like ACAS, as we shall see below, is often required for exam questions on employee relations processes.

Employee relations processes

The process of arbitration and why the parties (unions and employers) make use of this process to resolve their differences features regularly in exam questions. An essential point to remember is that although ACAS may be involved, there are also other independent arbitrators.

Other processes which have been the subject of exam questions include involvement through works councils, collective bargaining and agreements, and employee relations audits, for example:

> Discuss the view that collective bargaining is 'a good and desirable' employee relations process.

To obtain good marks in answering this question you would need to put points both in favour and against the view expressed. Collective bargaining is favoured by authors such as Allan Flanders and Neil Chamberlain because of its wage setting function, i.e. it establishes minimum rights for employees. On the other hand, collective bargaining is inflationary, can destroy jobs and make the labour market inflexible, and increases unit labour costs, all of which have an adverse impact on the product market competitiveness of enterprises. You should be able to provide examples from organisations to illustrate the desirable and not so desirable effects of collective bargaining.

Environmental context of employee relations

The role of government in employee relations and the implications of UK membership of the European Community are topics of current interest which feature regularly on the exam paper. The comparison between British systems of employee relations and other competitor countries is covered in the generalist module. An understanding of alternative approaches will help you to make a reasoned critical assessment of the context in which employee relations take place in the UK. Questions on this aspect of the syllabus could cover the Social Charter, or international bargaining, for example:

> 'Given the basis of trade union organisation in the UK and the rest of the European Community, it is unlikely that the advent of the European Single Market will see within the next five years the development of international bargaining.' To what extent would you agree with this statement?

To answer this you would need to show that you are aware of the differences between the basis of trade union organisation in the UK (job centred) and the remainder of the EC (religion, politics and, in Germany, industry). These would be a major obstacle to developing credible international trade union structures for bargaining with employers. In addition, many employer groups in Europe, including the CBI, and many multinational companies have strongly set their faces against international bargaining. So you would indicate the extent to which you agreed with the statement by giving examples drawn from both sides of the 'bargaining table'.

Section C: Employee relations skills

The questions in this section of the exam paper ask you about the skills required of an employee relations manager in handling different sorts of situations. These are typically negotiating, handling grievances and disciplinary cases and you will usually find a question on two if not all three of these areas. You should therefore find study and revision for this part of the exam paper relatively straightforward.

Negotiations

Questions on this topic can focus on a number of different aspects of the negotiating process: the types of negotiating situations in which a management team may find itself and the style of negotiation to use in different situations; considerations to take into account in selecting the team for bargaining with employee representatives; steps to take in preparing for negotiations; and techniques to use in a negotiating situation in order to find common ground and the basis of agreement. Sometimes a question could encompass several aspects as, for example, in this question.

> Your Chief Executive has decided that your organisation needs to introduce a management training course in negotiation skills. Write a report to the Chief Executive explaining what should be included in such a training course if it is to achieve its objectives, and why.

To answer this satisfactorily, you need to provide a definition of negotiations and indicate what should be included in the course, for example, the different types of negotiating situations (individual, grievance, bargaining, etc), the different stages that a set of negotiations go through, and therefore the skill requirements of a manager in each of these stages in the process. You must justify your proposals by explaining why these skills are critical to negotiators. An answer which merely lists a set of skills, for example interpersonal skills, judgemental skills, note-taking skills, would not gain a pass mark.

Handling grievances

The skills required by managers in handling employee grievances are frequently the subject of a question. It is important to recognise that good interviewing skills are crucial in order to gain information on the facts of a case, so that a manager can proceed through certain stages: analyse the grievance; establish aims in resolving the grievance; plan a strategy and tactics; present a case, and conclude agreement on resolution of the grievance.

Such questions will usually ask you to justify your answer, as for example in the following question:

> What skills do a management team need to have in preparing for handling an employee grievance, and why?

Too much description of the skills involved and insufficient attention to the 'why' part of the question would not lead to a pass mark.

Occasionally, a question may provide you with a specific situation, such as sexual harassment, and ask you how you would deal with it.

Disciplinary procedures

Questions on the topic of discipline can focus on the skills required by managers in handling discipline, in a similar way to the questions on grievances. In addition, they can focus on what is involved in drafting and introducing or reviewing a disciplinary procedure and occasionally questions may be concerned with preparing the organisation's case to present at an industrial tribunal in defence of a claim for unfair dismissal. Examples of questions would be as follows:

> What do you understand by the term 'best practice'? Why is it important for management when advising and operating a disciplinary procedure?

> Outline the process, and the skills required by management, in handling disciplinary matters. To what extent are these man-

agement skills different from those required of representatives of the employees?

You will note that this second question asks for a comparison between the skills of management and those of employee representatives. In the words of the examiner's report,

> The main causes of failure were that students simply listed the stages in a typical disciplinary procedure, did not answer the part of the question referring to the skills of the representative of the employee, or stated that the skills and role of the employee's representative at disciplinary hearings were different. The skills of the employee representative in terms of the preparation, presentation and concluding stages of disciplinary matters are exactly those of the management representative. It was surprising to be told by students that the role of the representative of the employee in disciplinary hearings was a passive one. The employee representative is at the disciplinary hearing to represent the employee in the same way as people have legal representatives in the legal system.

Other employee relations skills

Other situations which the employee relations manager might have to deal with include industrial action, handling the practical realities of achieving a single union agreement, as opposed to multi-union recognition, introducing a redundancy procedure or dealing with a redundancy situation. Any one of these could be included as a question. Also, the exam paper often has a general question which asks students to consider some issues and the skills involved, for example:

> Outline the characteristics of *three* of the following issues:
> – joint consultation
> – comparability
> – the 'bargaining ritual'
> – conciliation
> What skills are required by management in handling the issues you have selected?

The examiner's report illustrates the need to understand the precise sense of semi-technical terms if you decide to tackle such a question:

> Few candidates were able to explain the 'bargaining ritual'. They confused this with describing the negotiation process and then listing the skills required by negotiators. They failed to explain that the 'ritual' relates to formal presentation of claims and counter offers, long negotiating sessions, bluff and counter bluff and making agreements in the early hours of the morning etc.

The answers to such questions will require that you draw on your understanding of employee relations processes to provide a brief description of the issue, then explain the skills involved. It is not sufficient to just list the skills, you need to justify why these skills are required.

Types of Questions

The questions on the Employee Relations exam paper can take a variety of forms. You may be asked to recommend action in your 'own organisation', or a scenario may be presented and you are required to indicate how you would handle it. These types of questions are more likely to be found in the 'skills' section of the exam paper. Other questions are framed as essay-type questions, and usually have at least two parts which have to be answered. The guidance in Chapters 6 and 9 on tackling essay type questions will be worthwhile for you to read.

Where a question is set with separate parts, in many cases one part of the question may ask for a definition or descriptive answer, and the second part may call for some analysis and argument. In this case, more marks are likely to be awarded to the second part, although the possible marks will be reduced significantly if you do not answer the first part. Examples of questions of this type are given below:

> Outline and justify the circumstances in which you would consider advising your organisation to use the services of ACAS.

> Explain what you understand by the concept of 'the balance of bargaining power' and show, with appropriate illustrations,

how it might explain employee relations behaviour in the 1980s relative to the 1970s.

The latter question, according to the examiner's report, encouraged a range of simplistic responses: 'Very few were able to discuss the nature of bargaining power and few discussed technology as a factor which contributes to the balance of bargaining power. Most concentrated on economic and political factors. There was also much re-writing of the employee relations history of the 1960s and 1970s, particularly with respect to trade union/Labour Government relationships. However, most candidates sensibly discussed contrasts between the seventies and eighties.'

There is usually at least one question on the paper which asks you to present your answer in a particular format. This is often a report, but sometimes a question calls for a briefing paper or a training programme to be prepared. Where a report to higher management is indicated, marks will be awarded for addressing this requirement. The Chief Examiner has commented that you should give careful attention to the style of language you use in a report. Some students have written in a style that would give offence to senior management (for example, by questioning their ability and/or judgement) and which would in some companies result in severe disciplinary action, if not dismissal!

You should compose your answers from the standpoint of an employee relations manager. This means that you are expected to demonstrate that you understand the 'real world' of business and employee relations. For example, if you recommend that a private sector company should move from a multi-union situation to a single union situation, you should offer advice as to how to deal with the response and resistance of unions to such a move. Similarly if you propose the use of certain techniques and approaches, you should indicate why you consider they are appropriate to the problem or issue raised by the question, and explain the practicalities of their use in the situation.

There are many questions in which your answer will reflect your values, for example, for or against trade unionism. The examiners do not award marks for one set of values rather than another; what is important is whether you can support your conclusions by analysis and argument and whether the facts you use are correct.

In assessing answers to questions, the examiners are looking for the following:

- understanding of the subject and the issues.
- ability to apply, describe and analyse the appropriate management techniques.
- the understanding of the application of the management skills required to deal with problems.

Where an answer is borderline, the examiners use the following criteria in deciding whether it should pass or fail:

> The IPM Professional Qualification is an indication to employers that the holder of such a qualification can be reasonably expected to be *aware* and *informed* of the prevailing trends, topics and techniques in employee relations and human resource management and display an acceptable degree of proficiency in terms of the 'operational skills' that might be reasonably expected of a graduate member of the IPM . . .

So, for example, 'over the garden fence' type answers which lack objectivity or any evidence that the student has knowledge or competence to deal with the subject of the question in a constructive or critical way are to be avoided. Even if you have personal experience you should be able to comment on this critically and relate it to theories and concepts or the best practice advocated by employee relations practitioners.

The bottom line as far as the examiners are concerned is whether the answers you produce suggest that you could reasonably be left to work in a personnel department, relatively unsupervised, without causing mayhem!

Bibliography

ADAMSON, A. *A Student's Guide for Assignments, Projects, Field Studies and Research*. 3rd edition. Thamesman Publications in association with IPM, 1986.

BUZAN, T. *Use Your Head*. BBC Publications, 1975.

DUDLEY, G.A. *Rapid Reading – The high speed way to increase your learning power*. Thorsons, 1981.

HONEY, P. and MUMFORD, A. *The Manual of Learning Styles*. 3rd edition. Peter Honey, Maidenhead, 1992. (Available from: Ardingley House, 10 Linden Avenue, Maidenhead, Berks, SL6 6HB).

— *Using Your Learning Styles*. 2nd edition. Peter Honey, Maidenhead, 1986.

KOLB, D.A., RUBIN, I.M. and McINTYRE, J.M. *Organisational Psychology – an experiential approach*. Prentice Hall International, 1974.

PITFIELD, M. and DONNELLY, R. *How to Take Exams*. IPM, 1980.

ROWNTREE, D. *Learn How to Study*. Macdonald and Jane's, 1978.

SUTCLIFFE, G.E. *Effective Learning for Effective Management*. Prentice Hall, 1988.